D1560439

AARON SHEARER

CLASSIC
GUITAR
TECHNIQUE

VOLUME TWO

Franco Colombo
Publications

ISBN 0-89898-573-0

9 780898 985733

TABLE OF CONTENTS

FOREWORD

Volume I of *Classic Guitar Technique* presented a systematic approach for gradual musical and technical development toward mastery of this noble instrument. No effort has been spared in study, research, and experiment to continue the same approach in the present volume. The full value of these works will be grasped only by those students who are willing to contribute a similar effort on their own part, both in a sympathetic approach to the contents of the books, and a constant evaluation of personal problems which a text by its very nature is unable to consider. This text should be used with its supplements to coordinate a program of study that will comply with the requirements of the individual student.

A WORD OF CAUTION: The most harmful thing a student can do, both technically and musically, is to rush headlong into material that is beyond his stage of development. Some undesirable results of this mistake are:

1. He will establish a habit of error in both mind and muscles.
2. Harmful physical tension will result from attempts to drive muscles to do that for which they have not been gradually and carefully conditioned.
3. In the end, progress is actually *slower*. In fact, the more violent the attempt to master material without proper preparation the more harmful and frustrating is the final effect on the student.

The writer wishes to offer firm assurance to students who are willing to exert the effort: there is a way to approach music and the guitar in order to bring the two together in a unity of expression. The only requirements, beyond an ordinary amount of musical talent, is a plentiful measure of sincerity and self-discipline.

Rule Number 1 in study of the guitar is: KNOW ALL YOU CAN ABOUT AN EXERCISE OR COMPOSITION BEFORE YOU BEGIN TO PLAY. When beginning study of a piece or an exercise carefully consider the following details *before attempting to play*.

1. *Be able to count aloud and tap out fluently the rhythm* in at least a slow tempo, set and maintained by use of the metronome: Set the metronome as slowly as necessary; in certain instances double the time signature to establish a shorter note as the beat unit (explained in "Doubling the Time Signature" in the following article, Reading and Counting Rhythm). Refer to this article whenever doubt arises concerning rhythm.

2. *Always be aware of the purpose of an exercise.* Make sure that you know what particular area of development is being emphasized.

3. *Analyze the material for musical content:* What is the key (key signature) and in what position is it played? Acquire a clear mental picture of the location of the sharps or flats on the fingerboard. Does the material consist predominantly of chords, scales, or arpeggios, or do two of these, or all three appear? Analyze as fully as possible: scales, intervals, melody, harmony, chords, inversions, resolutions. If the student's level of development permits, an inner hearing of the music through sight-reading is always useful.

4. *What is the general fingering plan for both hands?* Look for left hand guide and pivot fingers, alternation or repetition of right hand fingers. *Which stroke is to be used— rest-stroke or free-stroke?* Is a change from one stroke to the other indicated?

After a careful analysis of the music, the next step is to consider how the material should be practiced.

The primary concern should be the matter of establishing habits of accuracy and continuity. *Guard against forming habits of error*. They become just as deeply ingrained as any other result of practice. When studying the guitar, two almost invariable rules should be observed:

1. NEVER PRACTICE MORE RAPIDLY THAN THE TEMPO AT WHICH YOU CAN PROCEED WITHOUT HESITATION AND ERROR.

2. EXTRACT PROBLEM PASSAGES AND STUDY THEM SEPARATELY UNTIL MASTERED.

Sometimes these passages prove to be excellent technical studies when analyzed and practiced out of context. Consider the time saved in isolating the difficult passages for special study. The writer sometimes hears a student repeat several measures over and over because of difficulty encountered in one measure or even on one beat. After several attempts, he finally succeeds in negotiating the passage once, then immediately proceeds to new material. A habit of error had been formed at that point in the music and it is almost certain that the error will occur at the next encounter. Make problem passages daily exercises. Repetition alone is not enough. Analyze the problem to learn *why* it is difficult. Include notes leading into and out of the difficult passage and master it to a level of fluency above that attained for the rest of the piece.

One other consideration: Is it a problem which may be solved with a reasonable amount of study or does it require overall development involving prolonged study? Has it served to point up a lack of knowledge in an important area of music or of the instrument, or a weakness in one hand or even one finger? Will it be better to review earlier studies to develop the area in which weakness is evident before attempting the piece in question again?

Important as these considerations are, there is another which dominates them all: SUSTAINED CONCENTRATION. Lack of it accounts for more wasted time and the development of more harmful muscular habits than any other factor. Long hours of rote practice and thoughtless repetition are harmful. Students sometimes suggest that muscles are developed by thoughtlessly thumping away at the strings, a highly dubious proposition at best. Muscles require direction in order to develop the intricate movement habits of playing. The longer and more intensely one is able to concentrate attention upon a specific subject, the more thoroughly *and* quickly all the particulars of the material are grasped and retained. There is nothing mysterious about learning to concentrate. The ability can be sharpened and developed over a period of time by approaching it correctly with a determined will. The author does not recommend attempting long periods of unbroken practice. If the mind begins to wander, stop working for a few minutes. Breathe deeply, walk around the room, think of something entirely different from what you are studying. Return to concentrate vigorously upon the study material in question, one problem at a time, knowing that correct habits of thought and execution are thus being formed. Divide practice sessions into several periods of a few minutes each in the beginning to permit short mental rests when necessary. Gradually lengthen the periods of study as the ability to concentrate develops. Proceeding in this manner will assure you of the most rapid progress possible toward realizing your full potential.

During the period of some five years since "Classic Guitar Technique", Volume I was completed, Volume II has been in varying stages of preparation. The material it contains is the result of constant inquiry into the problems of guitar instruction both as a private teacher and as a faculty member at American University—more lately at the Catholic University of America (where the guitar is considered a major instrument). Working in these capacities has brought me in contact with a vast cross-section of individuals interested in the guitar: students, some studying the guitar as an interesting diversion, others aspiring to instruct and perform on the highest level; teachers, many of whom have offered valuable suggestions. Each day I am reminded of my indebtedness to these individuals who have made it possible for me to formulate and test theories.

I wish to express deep appreciation to my pupil, Mr. Robert Luse, a young man possessing unusual analytical and teaching ability who is rapidly gaining recognition as a distinguished guitar instructor and performer. He has given freely of his time to read proof and has offered many valuable suggestions concerning clarification of the text.

Words of thanks fall far short of expressing my appreciation of the role of my wife, Virginia, in the writing of this book. Aside from the inspiration and understanding she has contributed to all I do, she applied herself generously to the long, tedious tasks of typing copy and pasting the manuscript together. Without her encouragement and assistance, I doubt that the work would have been written.

Aaron Shearer

Washington, D. C.

INTRODUCTION

The information and study material contained in *Classic Guitar Technique,* Volume I is a prerequisite to the proper study of the present Volume II. Although the reader may have played for a considerable period of time and feels that his knowledge and technique are adequate for work in this book, he should take time to examine the contents of Volume I carefully before proceeding. To use this book effectively the student must know correct seating with the guitar, right and left hand positions, use of the right fingers and thumb in rest-stroke and free-stroke, combinations of strokes between the thumb and fingers, strict alternation of fingers, and, of course, use of the left hand in executing all notes in the first position in scale, arpeggio, and chord study material. No special right hand instructions are presented in this volume (except in playing harmonics) because no basic right hand technical problems are to be found here which are not treated in Volume I.

The present work was written with the intention of presenting a nucleus of examples, exercises, and interesting, well-fingered pieces to provide a means for: (1) further general development of both hands, (2) learning the fingerboard throughout its full practical range, and (3) developing the student's general musical knowledge relative to the guitar.

However, the author does not imagine that all the music will be suitable for every pupil, especially where the study of chord formations is involved. The vast physical and mental differences among students make mandatory an individual approach to all material throughout this book. In using this text, the study of any material found to be impractical in particular cases should be deferred until further development permits profitable study. (Also, see page 14, "To The Teacher.")

If a progressive study of slurs and left hand reach development is not already under way, it should be begun immediately. These are highly important areas of left hand development which are thoroughly treated in the author's supplementary text, *Slur, Ornament, and Reach Development Exercises.*

Parallels

Apparently one reason for the previous absence of material for the study of basic chord formations has been fear of criticism from theorists about the voice leading which involves parallel octaves and fifths that inevitably occurs in exercises suitable for students at this level. The student must be first taught from the chordal schemes he can negotiate on the instrument. The elimination of all parallels in exercises during this phase of development would make the knowledge and execution of chord formations and their movements about the lower register impossible. This book disregards the prohibition on parallel voice leadings when it interferes with the effective presentation of study material.

Pivot and Guide Fingers

Using the techniques of pivot and guide fingers, as introduced in Volume I—and further elaborated in this work—will greatly facilitate left hand development. Smooth, unbroken playing often termed *legato* is the product of careful analysis of opportunities presented by each composition to use these devices. They offer the smoothest means of movement between notes—

where feasible they should be used as fully as possible. It should also be realized, however, that they may be carried to unnecessary extremes, resulting in a lack of mobility in the left hand. In general, pivot and guide finger techniques should be retained long enough to serve their purpose as connectors, and then discarded.

Throughout this book the indications for pivot and guide fingers are as follows:

1. The "hold" mark for a pivot finger is a short horizontal line; when placed after the finger number, (1-), it means that the 1st finger is held *through* a following passage. When placed before the finger number, (-1), it means that the 1st finger is held *from* a previous passage. Occasionally the hold mark is extended with a broken line to show *how long* the finger should remain down. (See exercise 1, page 10.)

2. The "glide" mark is a short line *set at an angle* to indicate that the guide finger glides along the string *to* another note upward, (2⁄), or downward, (2⧵); or *from* another note upward, (⁄2), or downward,(⧵2). (See *The Guide Finger Principle in Shifting*, page 104).

Concerning Use of the Strokes in Scales

Scale exercises should be played both rest-stroke (▾) and free-stroke (∪), using as many right finger combinations as time permits. The development of the free-stroke in scales will eventually be a significant aid in producing the more difficult arpeggio formations; it will also allow the student to play scales in situations where rest-stroke is not feasible.

The Importance of Instrument Adjustment

It is absolutely necessary that an instrument be in proper playing condition (see explanation and specifications, Volume I, *Classic Guitar Technique*). A very important factor in keeping the guitar in good playing condition is to have it tuned to *concert pitch at all times*; tuning too high can damage the instrument. Pitch inaccuracy, besides its self-evident incorrectness, also creates string tension adding unnecessary problems for both hands.

Supplementary Pieces

The section of supplementary pieces begins on page 145. A few of these pieces are relatively easy, others are difficult enough to require considerable study. They may be used either as material for further study or as recreation-pieces, depending upon the requirements and development of the student.

POSITION ON THE FINGERBOARD

One "position" on the fingerboard consists of four consecutive frets; a fret corresponding to each of the four left fingers. The "first position" includes open strings and notes on the first, second, third, and fourth frets, the "second position" contains the notes of the second, third, fourth, and fifth frets only, etc.

The specific fingerboard position in which the left hand plays at a given instance is determined by the fret upon which the 1st finger normally falls or would fall if used. A particular position is indicated by a Roman numeral written directly above the note or notes to be played in that position. An exception to the foregoing explanation of "position" relative to the left hand occurs when the 4th finger extends briefly to the adjacent higher position, or less frequently, when the 1st finger extends to the next position below. Extension into another position is, of course, a part of somewhat advanced fingering technique in which the normal position of the left hand is not appreciably altered.

IMPORTANT! Carefully distinguish between the use of Roman numerals when placed *above* the staff to indicate fingerboard position and when they are placed *below* the staff to identify chords as explained on page 15.

THE BAR

The bar in guitar technique refers to depressing more than one string simultaneously on a single fret with the 1st left finger as shown in Fig. 1. A cursory examination of several standard guitar editions produced the following array of designational systems for the bar: C (for Spanish *ceja*), ½CI, CI, CII, etc., Cl, ½Cl, ½C2, etc., c, c I, c3, etc., Ca, Ca7, Ca5ᵃ, Clᵃ, etc., and finally B (for French *barré*), including BI, BII, $_b^c$II, ½B.

The common fault of these systems is their failure to designate precisely the number of strings to be barred. In this text, bars will be designated as follows:

1. Capital B will precede a Roman numeral to indicate a six string bar in its proper position, as follows:
   (a) BI (six string bar at first position).
   (b) B IX (six string bar at ninth position)
2. When a bar of less than six strings is required, the capital B and Roman numeral will be followed by an encircled number corresponding to the last string covered by the first finger.
   (a) B III④ (third position bar across the first four strings)
   (b) B VIII⑤ (eighth position bar across the first five strings)
3. Chords requiring a partial bar permitting the first string to sound open will be notated by the most practical system in use: a bracket extending beside the notes to be covered with the bar finger; see the A Major chord below.

Correct execution of the full six string bar requires that the 1st finger press somewhat on its left side and extend very straight so that the pressure from each segment on the strings is as uniform as possible. Permit the left wrist to arch comfortably outward and the thumb to maintain its approximate position on back of neck almost opposite the 1st finger. (See Fig. 1.)

Discrete bar positions employing varying positions of the bar finger covering two, three, four, five and six strings must be cultivated in order to adjust discrepencies in the finger surface which hinder clear tone production. When less than six strings are barred, the bar finger may be permitted to bend slightly at the first and sometimes the second joint in accordance with the number of strings involved and the length of the performer's finger. The student should not expect to perform the bar with any degree of proficiency after only a few attempts, nor should he be discouraged when all strings do not readily sound clear. The necessary strength and control for the execution of this highly important area of guitar technique must be developed through much thought and patient practice.

CAUTION: Correct string adjustment is indispensible to proper bar development. (See page 2, The Importance of Instrument Adjustment).

Figure 1

Figure 2

Try the following F Major Chord requiring BI:
See Fig. 1.

Now try the following A7 Chord requiring BII④:
See Fig. 2.

The following A Major chord employs the partial bar which is designated by the bracket. This fingering requires that the second or tip-joint of the finger be collapsed; the tip-segment remains flat while the middle segment raises to clear the 1st string:

Chord Stroke with (p)

During the chord stroke the relationship between the thumb, hand and wrist should never be greatly altered from normal playing position. As in scales, the fused hand and arm pivot from the elbow, permitting the relaxed thumb to bounce across the strings. The left side of the wrist should rotate inward toward the strings so that the thumb, during a brief follow-through, will drop below the strings. Since considerable accent must usually fall upon the 1st string, the wrist is centered over that string at the culmination of the stroke.

The chord stroke with (p) is designated with a curved line placed to the left of the chord as follows:

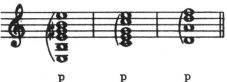

p   p   p

READING AND COUNTING RHYTHM

The first rule in reading rhythm is: *Always determine what element of the music—a note, a division of a note, a dot, or a rest—falls* ON EACH BEAT.

In counting rhythm, it is helpful to give each division of the beat a specific name. This gives the performer a ready means of identifying any division of the beat and placing it in proper rhythmic order.

Tap out each example using a pencil or a similar article, with a metronome set as slowly as is necessary to execute the rhythm properly. Finally, practice each rhythm example on an open string of the guitar until absolutely fluent; again use the metronome.

Do not neglect the most effective particular in the study of rhythms: COUNT ALOUD using numbers and syllables as explained in each example. Developing the habit of counting aloud fluently may require some practice but it is well worth the effort.

Counting Eighth Notes

The common practice of saying "and" (&) to the second of two eighth notes when the beat unit is a quarter note,

1 & 2 & 3 & 4 &

makes it a simple matter to count and play any rhythmic figure consisting of eighth notes (and rests), for example:

1 & 2 & 3 & 4 &   1 & 2 & 3 & 4 &

Eighth Note Arrangements with Dotted Quarter and Quarter Notes
(when the quarter note is the beat unit as in $\frac{2}{4}$, $\frac{3}{4}$, and $\frac{4}{4}$)

1. The dotted quarter note *on the beat*.
   The quarter note receives one full beat; the dot, which replaces the tie, falls upon the next beat; the eighth note is counted "&".

1 2   &   1 2 & 3   1   23 &   1 2   & 3 4   &

2. The eighth note *on the beat* followed by a dotted quarter note.
   Since the eighth note falls on the beat it must be followed by "&". Think of dividing the quarter note into two eighths, as follows:

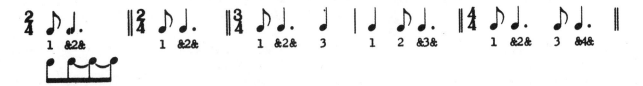

3. The eighth note *on the beat* followed by a quarter and another eighth *off the beat*.

   Notice the similarity between this figure and the one explained in the preceeding paragraph 2. The second eighth note replaces the dot; both may be counted in the same way. In this instance, also, think of dividing the quarter note off the beat into two eighths.

4. The following is an extension of the foregoing figure where the eighth note occurs on the beat and subsequent notes off the beat:

Counting Sixteenth Notes

When the beat unit is the quarter note and the beats are divided into sixteenth notes they are counted as follows:

1. Since the first and third sixteenths occupy the same positions within the beat as two eighth notes they are counted in the same manner:

2. The second and fourth sixteenths are given the specific syllabic names, "a" and "de," resulting in the following procedure for counting sixteenth notes:

3. Other sixteenth note arrangements:

Once the habit of counting is well established, unnecessary syllables should be dropped.

The student should count *on the beat* and *half beat* as soon as possible, and finally *on the beat only*.

Triplets

When the beat unit is the quarter note and the beats are divided into triplets they are counted:

Finally, the count may be simply:

⁶⁄₈ Time

When six eighth notes occur in a measure of ⁶⁄₈ time they are normally counted the same as triplets in ²⁄₄; they do not have the small "₃" marking:

Here, any similarity in counting $\frac{2}{4}$ and $\frac{6}{8}$ ends. The following rhythmic figures can not be written in $\frac{2}{4}$:

This is not a satisfactory way to count six sixteenth notes (sextuplets) or complex eighth note figures in $\frac{6}{8}$ time. Until the student has developed an advanced rhythmic sense and can feel the triplet figure in varying arrangements, sextuplets (six notes per beat), and other figures involving sixteenth notes in $\frac{6}{8}$ time, he is strongly advised to consider the eighth note as the beat unit and count accordingly, as follows:

Doubling the Time Signature

When playing at a slow tempo it is often helpful to double both numbers of the time signature and count twice the number of beats per measure. For example, set the metronome at ♩ = 42 and try to tap out the following rhythm:

Obviously, it is much easier to count and maintain an even tempo by doubling the time signature and metronome setting. The eighth note then becomes the beat unit to receive one count and the metronome is set at ♪ = 84:

Watch for slow pieces in $\frac{2}{4}$, $\frac{3}{4}$, and $\frac{4}{4}$ containing passages of eighth and sixteenth notes, and especially dotted eighths and sixteenths. They are often played better and more easily by doubling the pulse unit and counting four in $\frac{2}{4}$, six in $\frac{3}{4}$, and either two fours or eight in $\frac{4}{4}$.

Thirty-second and Dotted Sixteenth Notes

When the pulse unit is an eighth note, as in ⅜ time, thirty-second and dotted sixteenth notes are counted the same as sixteenths and dotted eighths when the pulse unit is a quarter note:

When the pulse unit is a quarter note, it is advisable to double the time signature and pulse rate as recommended in the preceding section; the following simplified counting will result:

THE KEY OF C MAJOR*

The C major scale is as follows:

Memorize the complete scalewise progression of notes, Key of C Major, first position. Begin and end with the Tonic (Key Note) C:

Ex. 1

(Hold finger down)

When the foregoing can be played from memory at least three times in succession at an even tempo without hesitation, practice it in 8th notes, counting, 1 & 2 &, two notes to each beat. Begin with the metronome set very slow and gradually work up to at least M.M. 84. The numbers 1 and 2 are spoken ON the beat (click of the metronome), the syllable "&" precisely between.

Ex. 2

The student is urged to pursue diligently further study of scales. A thorough study of scales, scale patterns, and rhythms is absolutely essential for rapid and positive progress in learning to read and play well.

———————

*For a thorough explanation of the Major and minor Keys, see <u>Basic Elements of Music Theory</u>, Shearer.

Folk Dance

1. Notes with stems up, all rest-stroke (▾) with fingers.
2. Bass notes (stems down), all free-stroke (◡) with (p) and where indicated, with (i).
3. Notice that each group of 8th notes begins with (m) except at the 13th measure.

Country Dance

1. Notes with stems up, all rest-stroke with fingers.
2. Bass notes (stems down), all free-stroke with (p) and where indicated, with (i).
3. *Hold all basses for full duration.*

Allegretto M.M. ♩ = 112   A.S.

Canonic Etude in C

A musical composition wherein one part is imitated note for note in another part is called a *canon*. Several measures of the following piece contain such passages of strict imitation, i.e., measures 2, 10, 14, and 18 where the treble part of the preceding measure is imitated in the bass.

1. All canonic measures, treble (notes with stems up), rest-stroke with fingers; bass (stems down), free-stroke with (p).
2. Arpeggio passages, i.e., measures 3—4, 7—8, 11—12, etc. all free-stroke.

CHORDS

A chord is a group of at least three tones which blend harmoniously when played together. In order to acquire necessary facility in use of chords, it is of the utmost importance that the student learn to identify them by name. To give the complete name of a chord is to reveal much about its construction and musical function. There are three steps to naming a chord correctly. All three means of identification are commonly used; all three are absolutely necessary to the music student and must be learned thoroughly.

1. A chord is named according to the *letter-name of its root* (the note upon which it is based): C, G, F♯, B♭, etc. The problem is knowing which note of a chord is its root since the root does not always occupy the same relative position within a chord. It may be the lowest note, the highest note, or a note between.

2. A chord is named according to the *intervals* it contains, giving it a harmonic name: major, minor, augmented, or diminished. This step in naming a chord obviously requires a basic knowledge of intervals and their use in chord construction.

3. A chord is named according to the *scale-degree name of its root:* I or tonic, IV or subdominant, V or dominant, etc. Since a particular chord does not occupy the same place and position of importance in all scales, a thorough familiarity of *scales in chords* (triads) is necessary to accomplish this highly important step in naming a chord.

Precise definitions of all the above are furnished in the author's companion volume to this work, *Basic Elements of Musical Theory*. This writer does not consider it practical to combine in one book an intensive study of theory with performance techniques. The study of chords which follows is therefore limited to that which can be coherently related to the manual element of playing. An understanding of the theory of music is indispensable to complete mastery of any instrument, however, and the use of *Basic Elements of Musical Theory* is energetically recommended.

TO THE TEACHER

The following material involving the study of chords is not intended for all students and need not be presented exactly in the given order. Very young students and those with small or underdeveloped hands will have extreme difficulty executing certain chord formations. In such cases, prohibitively difficult material may be given either a thorough or cursory explanatory inspection in accordance with the interest and perception of the student; actual playing is minimized with the understanding that it will be practiced later. The statement appearing in the Introduction concerning this and similar situations which may occur is re-emphasized: Any material found to be impractical in particular situations should be deferred until the student's development permits useful study.

THE MAJOR KEY—The Primary Chords

As the name implies, the primary chords of a key form the most important chord group in music. They serve to establish the key of a composition, constitute a general harmonic basis for most music, and are the entire harmonic content of countless, simple, well known songs.

The ability to recognize the primary chords by sound, by sight, and by formation on the fingerboard is of utmost importance to the guitarist; they furnish familiar guideposts along the way in reading, understanding, learning, and finally performing even complicated music.

1. The TONIC, designated by the Roman numeral I placed *below* the chord, called the "one chord", is based upon the 1st degree (key note) of the scale.
2. The SUBDOMINANT or IV ("four chord") is based upon the 4th degree of the scale.
3. The DOMINANT or V ("five chord") and DOMINANT 7th or V7 ("five-seven chord") are based upon the 5th degree of the scale.

The Primary Chords—Key of C Major

The letter-name of each chord coincides with the scale-degree which constitutes the chord-root; *capital* letters C, F, and G indicate major chords. The basis for all chord formations is the *Triad*. The following triads are in *root position*, i.e., with the root as the bass (lowest) note:

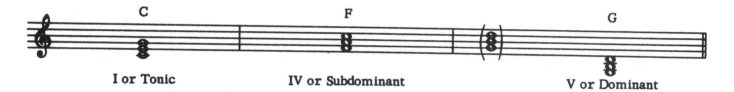

I or Tonic   IV or Subdominant   V or Dominant

Basic Chord Formations

Any note of a triad may be doubled an octave higher or lower to build complete basic chord formations on the guitar. *The name of the chord remains the same.* Full basic chord formations contain commonly used three-note, four-note, five-note, and six-note groups which constantly furnish the guitarist points of reference in performing all tonal music.

The following basic chord formations should be thoroughly memorized. Execute slow *chord-stroke* with "p" (see page 4); each tone should ring clearly:

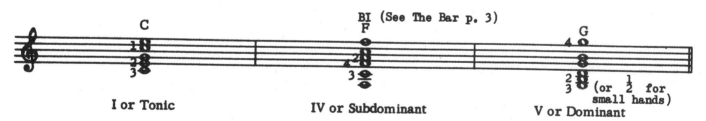

I or Tonic   IV or Subdominant   V or Dominant

G7, called "G seventh" or more correctly "G dominant seventh", indicates a G Major chord to which has been added the note "F", creating an interval of a 7th (counting upward, the root "G" through "F").

V7 or Dom. 7th

The dominant and dominant 7th chords serve essentially the same purpose within a key. Their difference lies in the fact that the dominant 7th is dissonant, strongly demands resolution, and more actively establishes a "key feeling". Because of this and because of its extremely common use, the dominant 7th will appear more frequently than the dominant in this book.

16

Memorize the foregoing chords and practice the following exercise with (p) chord-stroke.

Set M.M. slow and *maintain even tempo*; hold each chord as long as possible before changing to the next formation.

Ex. 3

(hold)

INVERSION OF CHORDS

When the *root* of a chord is *not its lowest (bass) note* the chord is said to be inverted. Notes of a chord may be rearranged in varying ways to produce inversions. Any note of a chord can be its bass or highest voice, but the *root* and *name of the chord* remain the same.

Root Position and Inversions of Triads

The three notes of a triad may be disposed in three different ways: root position, 1st inversion, and 2nd inversion.

The small Arabic number placed at the lower right side of a Roman numeral indicates 1st inversion or 2nd inversion:

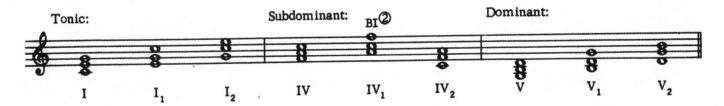

Tonic: Subdominant: Dominant:

I   I₁   I₂   IV   IV₁   IV₂   V   V₁   V₂

Four Voice Root Positions and Inversions of the Three Principal Chords

In a similar manner, notes from basic chord formations are employed to produce inversions. Compare inversions with the root position basic chord formations shown in parenthesis.

---

*See discussion of parallels in teaching chords on the guitar, page 1.

Notice that some tones have been deleted, others doubled, so that the chords sound well on the guitar:

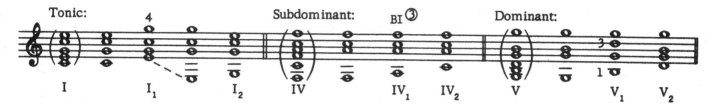

Since the dominant 7th consists of *four* different scale degrees it occurs in *four* positions:

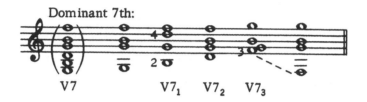

Exercises with the Primary Chords in Root Position and Inversion

Ex. 4

Ex. 5

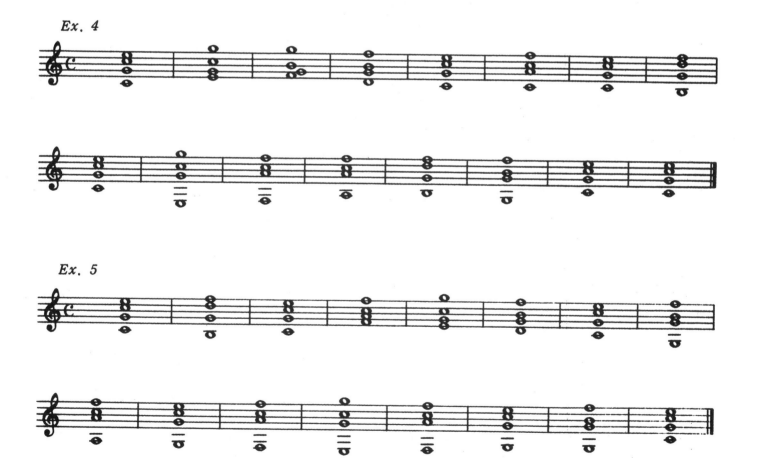

Rhythm forms for studying the above exercises: Concerning d. and e., refer to "Sixteenth Notes" in the preceding section, Reading and Counting Rhythm, page 6.

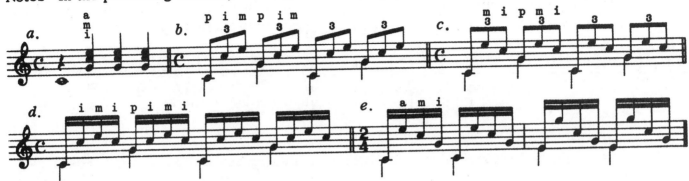

All exercises involving (p), (i), and (m) must also be practiced thoroughly with (p), (m), and (a); (m) replaces (i), and (a) replaces (m). DO NOT NEGLECT THE TRAINING OF (a)!

The highest note of a chord is often found on the 2nd string; it occurs less frequently on the 3rd.

Notice that all of the following are derived directly from or are closely related to the basic chord formations shown above:

Exercises with the primary chords, root position and inversion, highest note on the 2nd string: Use same rhythm forms as for Exercise 4.

Ex. 6

Ex. 7

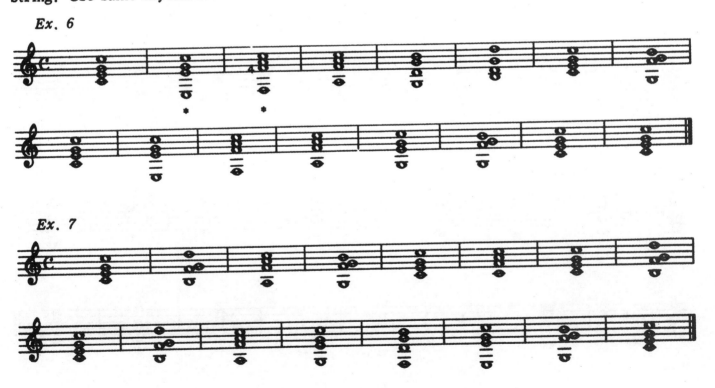

The following *Prelude* is an example of how chords other than the primary chords are used to create appealing harmonic progressions. Two of the primary chords are present, however; look for them. No metronome marking is included. The composition may be played as rapidly as the development permits. *CAUTION: Never sacrifice evenness and clarity for speed!*

Prelude in C

M. Carcassi

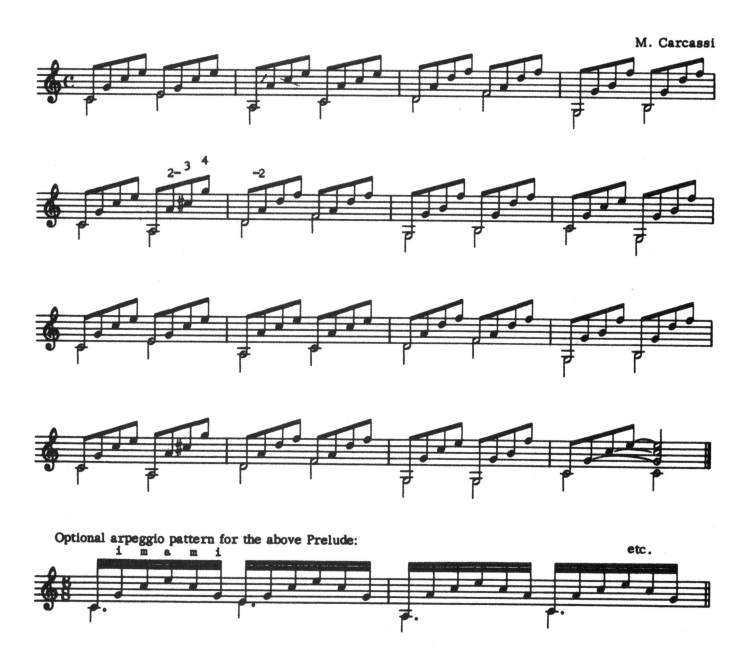

Optional arpeggio pattern for the above Prelude:

The following *Etude* and short piece should be practiced very slowly at first. Isolate difficult chord changes and practice them separately. Fluent execution of chords can be developed only through repetition. These pieces should not be neglected if they seem difficult; they are worth the effort required to perfect them.

Etude

Eventide

Nocturne contains some of the more common foreign terms and abbreviations used to indicate interpretation. In order to acquire a vocabulary of these terms, the student should own a dictionary of musical terms and use it often.

Notice the crescendo ⟨ and decrescendo ⟩ signs (called "wedges") below the staff. Although they appear in only the first four measures, they indicate the general dynamic treatment of the piece throughout. This is the meaning of the abbreviation "sim." (simile) at measure 5.

Nocturne

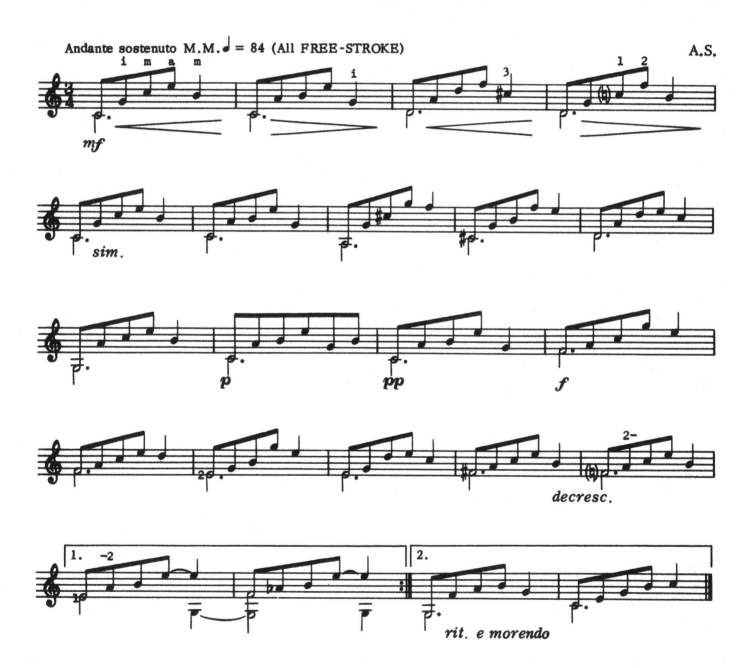

Petite Chanson

Never attempt to play a piece until you can count it and tap it out fluently with the metronome.

Begin the following *Moderato* by Carulli very slowly. If the dotted quarter notes are difficult to count, review the section Reading and Counting Rhythm. Practice with the metronome until a positive, steady tempo can be maintained—particularly at the abrupt transition from eighth to sixteenth notes.

Moderato

M.M. ♩ = 88

F. Carulli

Additional pieces in the key of C Major appear in the supplementary section beginning on page 145.

THE MINOR KEY

There are two commonly used forms of the *minor scale:*

1. The *harmonic minor* from which "harmony" or chords in the minor key are derived:

Note that the 7th degree of the scale is raised chromatically creating a 1½ step interval between 6 and 7, and a half-step between 7 and 8. These are the distinguishing characteristics between the *harmonic minor* and the *natural minor* scale, which has no accidentals.

2. The *melodic minor* scale is most frequently found in melodies. Carefully observe the difference between the *ascending* and *descending* forms:

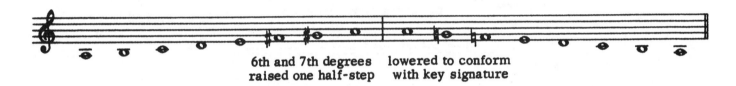

6th and 7th degrees   lowered to conform
raised one half-step   with key signature

The ascending melodic minor scale has the 6th degree raised in order to eliminate the 1½ step interval, which is somewhat awkward to sing, between the 6th and 7th degrees. However, since no such difficulty exists for instrumentalists the harmonic minor scale, also, is often used melodically in non-vocal music.

The student guitarist should spare no effort to become fluent in performing both forms of the minor scale. Play and sing both forms several times until you are able to distinguish between them.

The Key of A Minor

(Relative to C Major)

The keys of C Major and A Minor have the same key signatures (no sharps or flats); they are therefore referred to as *related keys*. The key of A Minor is the *relative minor* to C Major; C Major is the *relative major* to A Minor.

Memorize the following A melodic minor scalewise progression of notes using the first and briefly the second position. The shift is necessary in order to play A on the 5th fret, first string.

SHIFTING: Minimize the tendency for the left thumb to drag along the neck in shifting. Release pressure for an instant so that the thumb will slide along the neck—it will thus maintain the same position relative to the fingers at all times. In the following exercises the shift is precisely the distance between the first and second frets. It is executed while the 1st open string is played as the scale ascends, and an instant before playing G (on 1st string) in descending.

Remember, an accidental is effective only for the duration of the particular measure in which it appears.

Ex. 8

When Exercise 8 can be played from memory without hesitation, study it in 8th notes in $\frac{3}{4}$ time. The student will find that it is necessary to play the exercise completely through three times without pause for it to come out even; i.e., for the beginning A to re-occur on the first beat of the measure.

Check alternation of R.H. fingers: in counting 1 & 2 & 3 &, be certain that the beginning finger plays on the beat, the alternate finger on "&" throughout the exercise. Use i-m throughout, then m-a, then m-i, then a-m. *Do not neglect fingers m-a and a-m!*

Use the metronome to check tempo; it should be used until even tempo can be maintained.

Ex. 9

26

An exception to the general rule of strict alternation of R.H. fingers is found in the following *Etude*; (i) is repeated at the beginning of each phrase following a single quarter note. This eliminates an awkward R.H. fingering that would occur on the third to the first beats of measures 3 and 4 respectively.

Etude

Study the following A Harmonic Minor scale exercises as you did the melodic minor exercises.

Ex. 10

Optional fingering— 3   4   3

Ex. 11

28

Caravan

The predominantly scalewise center section (measures 15-30) is played rest-stroke, the rest of the piece free-stroke.

Allegretto M.M. ♩ = 100

A.S.

mf

f

mf

f

p

ff

p

morendo

The Primary Chords—Key of A Minor

The I or tonic is A Minor.

The IV or subdominant in D Minor.

The V or dominant is E Major; V7 or dominant 7th is E7.

NOTE: Small letters are used to identify minor chords; capital letters denote Major and Dominant 7th chords:

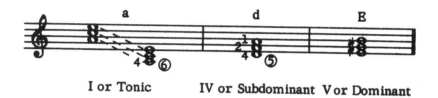

I or Tonic   IV or Subdominant V or Dominant

Basic Chord Formations

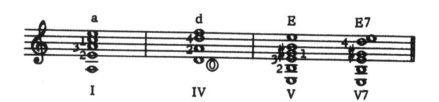

I   IV   V   V7

Memorize the foregoing chords and practice the following exercise, "p" chord-stroke:

Ex. 12

Root Position and Inversions of the Primary Chords

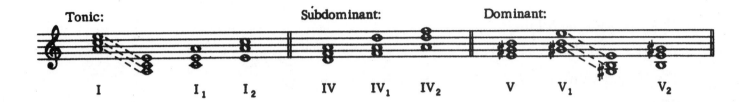

Tonic: I   I₁   I₂   Subdominant: IV   IV₁   IV₂   Dominant: V   V₁   V₂

Four-Voiced Chord Formations:

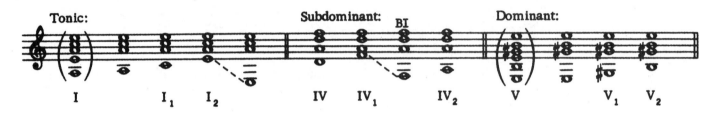

Tonic: I   I₁   I₂   Subdominant: IV   IV₁   IV₂   Dominant: V   V₁   V₂

Dominant 7th:

Ex. 13

Arpeggio patterns for the above:

Root position and inversions with the highest note on the 2nd string: The IV (root position D Minor) is included for the sake of completeness. It should not be played at this time. The V7₁ (E7 first inversion) must be learned thoroughly.

Chord Study– Key of A Minor

Rhythm forms for studying the above:

Waltz in A Minor

Moderato M.M. ♩ = 100
The entire piece is played FREE-STROKE.

A.S.

In ⁶⁄₈ time the customary beat unit is ♩. . Correctly counted at ♩. = 40 in the following piece, however, it is too slow for a steady rhythmic feeling. A better procedure therefore is to count six beats to the measure with M.M. ♪ = 120. Observe all rests in the bass part with the utmost care. When necessary, place (p) back on string to stop vibrations.

Siciliana

Adagio (All FREE-STROKE)

F. Carulli

34

Etude in A Minor makes use of an effective device for lending dissonant contrast to a composition. The eleventh measure of the second section contains the repeated bass note, A, below the V and V7 harmonies.   This is known as a pedal or organ point.*   Played reasonably fast and with continuity, the passage sounds well.

Etude in A Minor

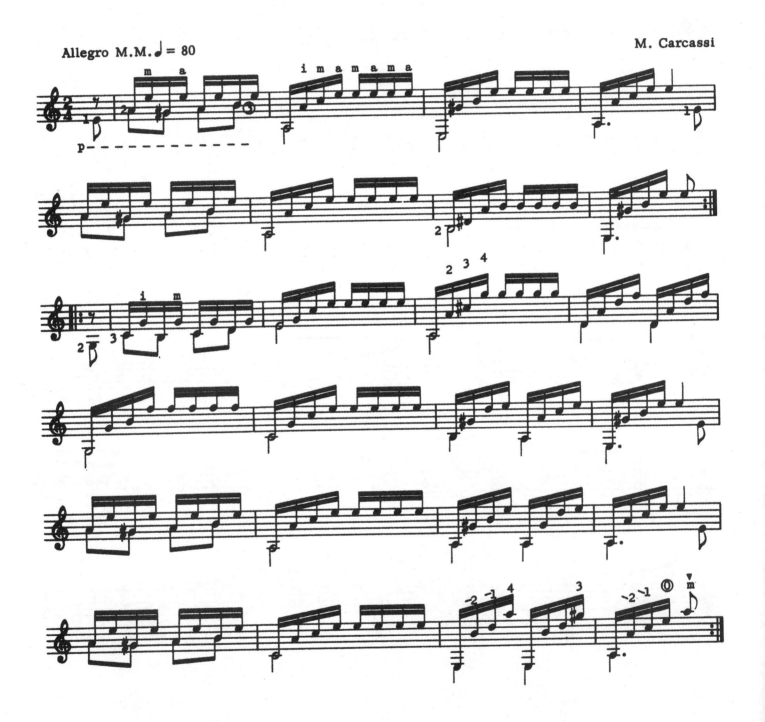

*Consult dictionary for definitions of these terms.

The following piece is an excellent study for the training of (m) and (a). Left hand fingering includes use of the slurs in all scale passages, and these should be executed carefully and exactly. (It is assumed that the student has already begun the study of *slurs*. See page 1, paragraph 4.)

Allegretto in A Minor

M.M. ♩ = 108
(All scale passages REST-STROKE)

F. Carulli

Additional pieces in the key of A Minor appear in the supplementary section beginning on page 145.

THE KEY OF G MAJOR

The sharp appearing on the 5th or "F" line of the staff is the G Major Key Signature. This indicates that F♯ instead of F is played throughout regardless of the octave in which it appears.

Two full octaves of the G Major Scale are available on the guitar in the first position.

Memorize the following:

Ex. 15

Ex. 16

Waltz of the West

A.S.

cresc.

38

The following piece begins as a canon in two parts. Carefully bring out the imitation of the theme in the bass.

Lullaby in G

Little Song

Andante M.M. ♩ = 76   A.S.

(optional)

The Primary Chords—Key of G Major

The key of G Major contains only one new group of chord formations: the V or *Dominant* D and D7 formations.

The tonic or I in G, which is, of course, the G Major chord, was V in the key of C Major.

The subdominant in G, which is the C Major chord, was I in the key of C Major.

Both the G and C Major chords are included here for completeness and especially for the purpose of review in a different key. The student should spare no effort, through careful listening and repetition, to become thoroughly familiar with these chords in their new positions within the key.

Triads:

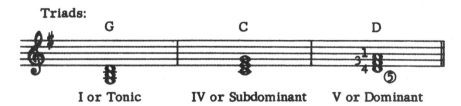

G	C	D
I or Tonic	IV or Subdominant	V or Dominant

Basic Chord Formations

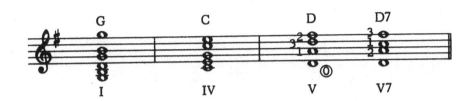

Memorize thoroughly the V and V7 (D and D7) formations before proceeding to the following exercise. ("p" Chord-Stroke)

Ex. 17

Many chords have optional fingerings. The fingering indicated in any given case is the one which makes the chord the easiest within a particular passage.

The following four fingerings for D Major are used throughout this book; try each in the preceding exercise:

Root Position and Inversions of the Three Principal Chords

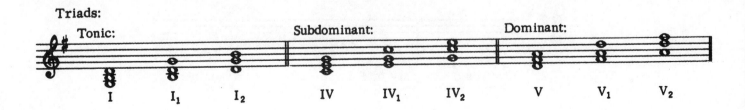

Four-voiced Chord Formations:

Tonic: Subdominant: Dominant:

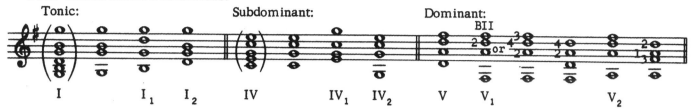

I I_1 I_2 IV IV_1 IV_2 V V_1 V_2

Ex. 18

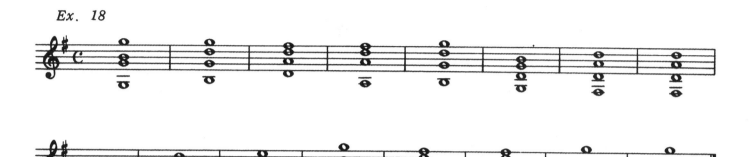

Dominant 7th: (The $V7_2$ chords shown below are spoken of as "incomplete" because their root is missing.)

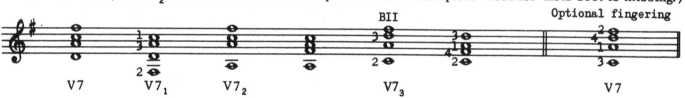

V7 $V7_1$ $V7_2$ $V7_3$ V7

Ex. 19

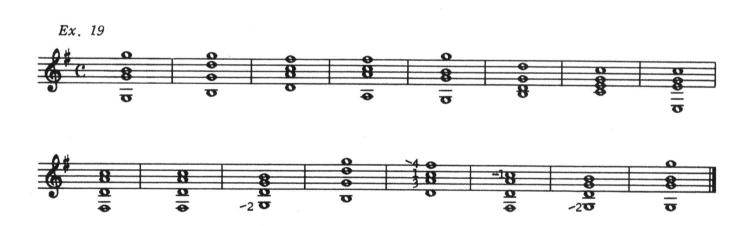

Rhythm forms for studying both the above exercises:

42

Ex. 20 (Employing V7₃ formations)

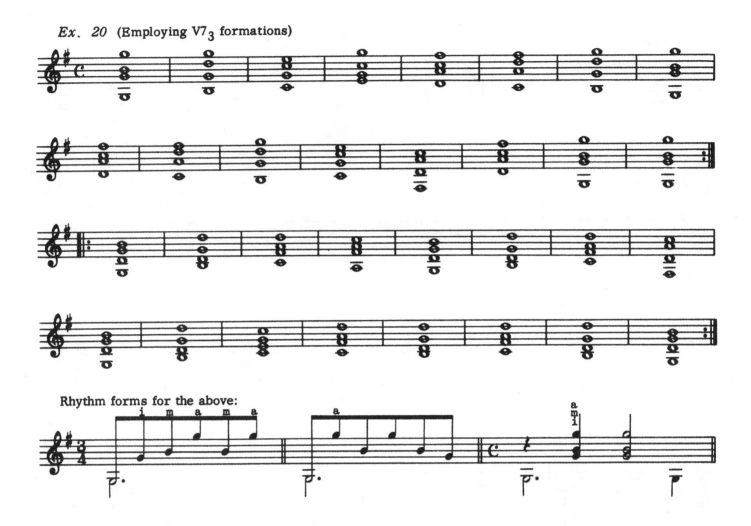

Rhythm forms for the above:

The following composition—and five other pieces in different keys which appear in later pages—were written especially for this book by the composer-teacher-guitarist George Yeatman. The composer has cleverly employed contemporary harmony to capture the colorful sounds of the music of today.

The wavy line found at the left of the final chord means that the chord is to be played broken or arpeggiated. The sign ⌒ indicates a *fermata*, or "hold".

Prelude in G Major

Moderato

G. Yeatman

44

Barcarolle

Andantino M.M. ♩.= 56

Melody rest-stroke; bass free-stroke entirely with (p)

M. Carcassi

Andante

Grazioso M.M. ♩ = 60
(All FREE-STROKE)

F. Carulli

Spring Song

Moderato M.M. ♩ = 88
(All FREE-STROKE)

A.S.

mp

ff

f   *mp*

poco rit.

The Key of E Minor

(Relative to G Major)

As is the case with its relative major, there are two full octaves of the E Minor scale available in the first position:

E Melodic Minor Scale:

The complete scalewise progression of notes in the first position; to be memorized.

Ex. 21

E Melodic Minor Scale Exercise:

Remember: An accidental is effective only for the duration of the particular measure in which it appears.

Ex. 22

E Harmonic Minor Scale - In complete first position:

Ex. 23

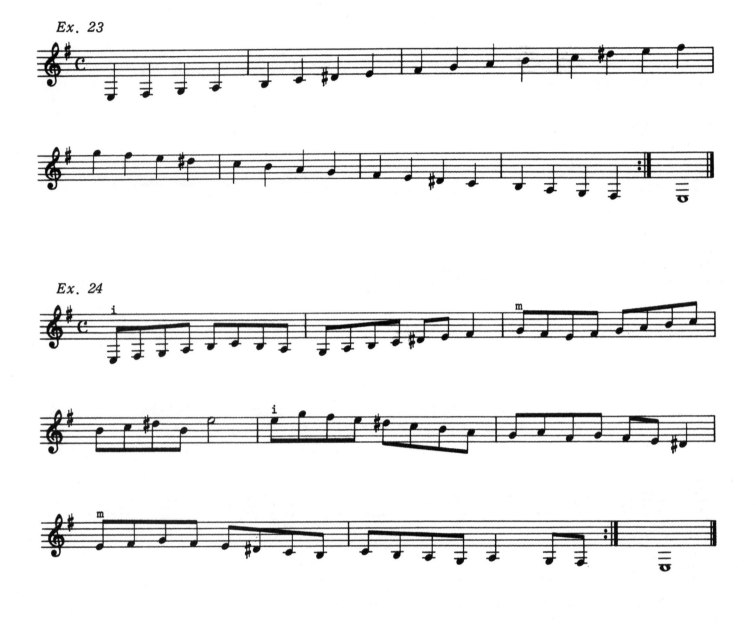

Ex. 24

The Primary Chords—Key of E Minor

The I or tonic is E Minor

The IV or subdominant is A Minor (same as I in the Key of A Minor).

The dominant and dominant 7th are B Major and B7.

Triads:

Basic Chord Formations

The V (B Major) chord is shown for reference only—this formation is extremely difficult for most students at the present level of development. It may be learned later when it will again be presented in another key.

Ex. 25

Root Position and Inversions of the Three Principal Chords

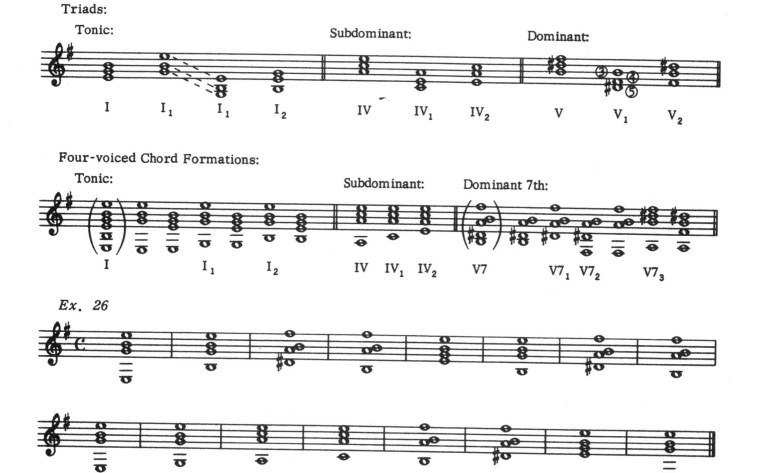

50

Ex. 27

Ex. 28 (Use rhythm form c. below)

Rhythm forms for studying the above:

Count the treble and bass parts separately in the following *Allegretto*. Notice that although some bass notes have been written a little to the right of treble notes occurring on the first beat of the measure, they are sounded together.

Observe rest-stroke and free-stroke signs.

Allegretto

M.M. ♩ = 144

F. Carulli

Fine

D.C. al Fine

Prelude in E Minor

A.S.

Moderato M.M. ♩ = 76

As in the preceding Carulli piece, *Andante* by Sor contains basses which are not written in line with their treble notes rhythmically; see 3rd and 14th measures in the second section. Count each voice separately to determine that the melody and bass are sounded together. Count and tap out the 8th and the next to last measures before attempting to play.

The ornamental *acciaccaturas* appearing in measures 2, 6, and 19 (marked *) require special attention. For complete explanation, see the author's book entitled *Slur, Ornament, and Reach Development Exercises*.

Andante

Etude in E Minor

G. Yeatman

HARMONICS

There are two kinds of harmonics, those produced on an open string called *natural harmonics*, and those produced on a stopped string called *artificial harmonics*.

Natural Harmonics

A harmonic is produced by touching a vibrating string lightly at a point of exact division (one-half, one-third, one-fourth, one-fifth the string length) forming *nodes* or points along the string which are stationary or free of vibration.

A node at one-half the string length.

A harmonic played at the 12th fret forms a node which divides the vibrations of the string into halves. This produces a pitch exactly one octave above the open string—the same as the string depressed at the 12th fret.

Observe the following steps in playing the harmonic at the 12th fret; it may be done on any string, but the E-6th is usually easier to begin:

1. A left hand finger is held somewhat extended to touch the string directly over the fret lightly with palmar surface of finger.

   CAUTION: DO NOT DEPRESS STRING.

2. The nodal point occurs where the 12th fret would touch the string; the left finger used to form the node *takes the place of the fret* and must not touch the string *back* of the fret as in ordinary playing.

3. Sound the string quite forcefully with (p) midway between the soundhole and bridge; lift the left hand finger the instant vibrations from the string are felt.

There will be a tendency to muffle the vibrations by touching the string too long, or to sound the open string by lifting the finger too soon. This must be overcome through careful practice and analysis of the technique described above—the only way of acquiring the coordination necessary to execute harmonics with precision and confidence.

Follow the same procedure for playing the 12th fret harmonics on each of the five remaining strings.

The pitch is raised as the number of string vibration division increases. As just explained one node at the 12th fret divides the string vibrations into two equal segments, producing the octave.

The next higher harmonic is played at either the 7th fret or the 19th fret, forming two nodes which divide the vibrations of the string into three equal segments. This produces a tone at the interval of a perfect fifth above the preceding octave.

The next higher harmonic may be played at either the 5th fret or at the point where the 24th fret would be found if the fingerboard were extended. This forms three nodes which divide the vibrations into four equal segments producing a tone exactly two octaves above the open string.

The highest harmonic commonly used on the open strings of the guitar is played slightly to the left of either the 4th, 9th, or 16th frets (and also at the point where the 28th fret would be found on an extended fingerboard). This forms four nodes which divide the string vibrations into five segments producing an interval of a major third above the preceding two-octave harmonic.

Occasionally the next higher harmonic, played somewhat to the right of the 3rd fret and having five nodes, is found in guitar music. Further harmonic divisions of the strings of the guitar produce such weak tones that they are generally considered impractical.

No standard system of notating harmonics exists in either instructional works or other publications for the guitar. The procedure most used is that of writing the abbreviation "Harm" or "Arm" (from Sp. *Armonicos*) and the fret number above or below an open string. Occasionally a composer (e.g., H. Villa-Lobos) employs a system similar to that commonly used to notate harmonics in violin music. Diamond shaped notes are written according to the fret and string involved (not the actual pitch of the harmonic), and regular notes (actual pitch). No notation of harmonics in common use, however, gives the performer a ready view of the actual tone intended by the composer. In the interests of consistency the author has established the following system for notation for this work:

1. Diamond shaped notes (◇, ♩, ♪,) are used to indicate all harmonics. This eliminates the necessity of writing "Harm" above or below the note, and calls attention more immediately to those notes to be played as Harmonics.
2. All harmonics are written *as they actually sound* with ledger lines or the *8va* sign when necessary.
3. Natural harmonics, which are played on open strings, are accompanied by the usual ⓪.
4. String (encircled Arabic numbers) and fret (Roman numerals) numbers are used when necessary to indicate the location of the harmonic.

The following table of natural harmonics shows that, of the four harmonics on each string which are most commonly used, only those on the 5th and the 9th frets actually require fret indications; all others coincide in *letter-name* with the notes found at those frets. Harmonics at the 7th fret sound one octave higher than the point where they are played, and those at the 4th fret two octaves higher. All harmonics at the 12th and the 19th frets coincide in letter-name and pitch with the notes found at those frets. Complete markings are provided, however, in cases where there can be a question.

Harmonics on the lower strings are usually sounded with (p); those on the higher strings with the fingers. But this is entirely a matter of convenience and it should be understood that (p), (i), (m), or (a), may play *any* string whenever advantageous.

Very high harmonics are more distinct and are more readily produced when sounded near the bridge, and struck with considerable force.

Table of Natural Harmonics

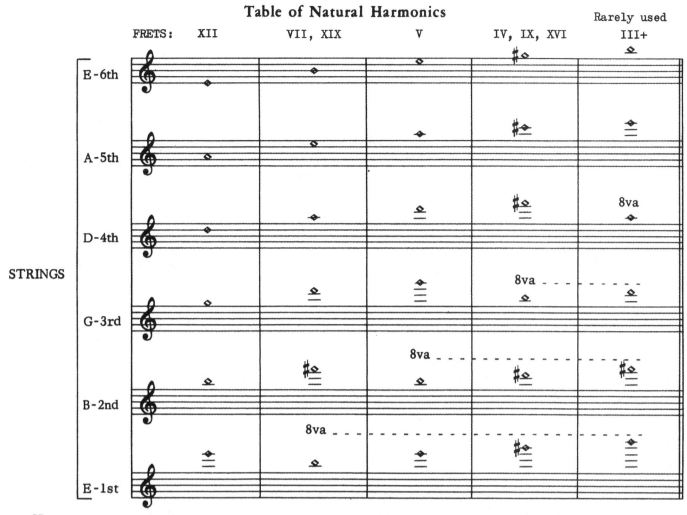

Harmonics may be executed singly or in groups of two or more together. Be sure to extend L.H. finger so that it touches the strings with its palmar surface, not with the extreme tip.

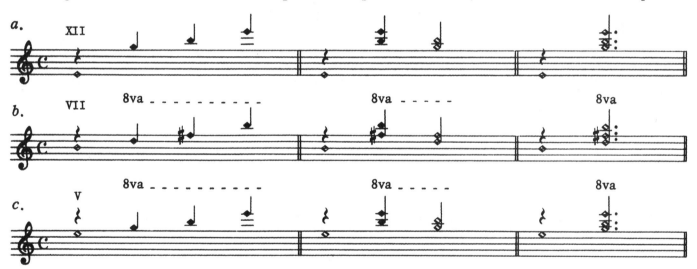

Etudes in Natural Harmonics

The Harmonic, A, found in the 3rd and 11th measures of the following *Etude* is played with (p) free-stroke; all other harmonics to the 19th measure are played with (a) rest-stroke. The E minor arpeggio in harmonics at the 19th and the 21st measures are played (a) (m) (i) rest-stroke. The three notes of the final chord are touched with the 4th finger and are played with (i) (m) (a) or (p) (i) (m). All chords (except the final one, of course) are played in the first position. Care must be exercised to play them *sotto voce*, or subdued, in order not to obscure the melody in harmonics. These chords are more effective if played slightly *staccato,* by placing the R.H. fingers back on the strings soon after they are sounded.

First practice the harmonics alone, in even rhythm, or better, commit them to memory; then include the chords.

Two Harmonic Etudes in E Minor

Harmonic Etude in G Major

A.S.

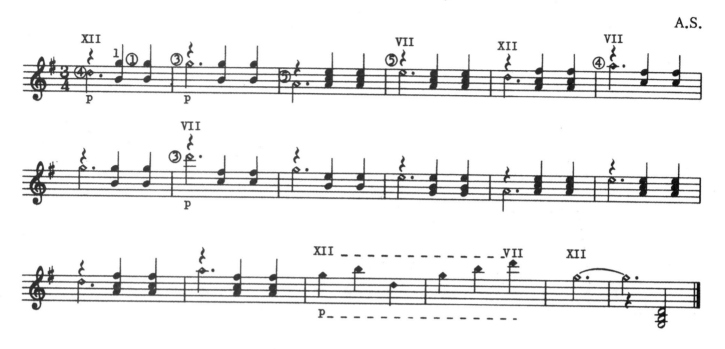

Right Hand Harmonics

Another technique of producing natural harmonics involves the right hand alone. The (i) finger is extended forward to touch the string at the proper fret and the harmonic is sounded either by (p) Figure 3, or by (a) Figure 4. The (i) finger is lifted outward slightly, immediately after sounding the harmonic with (p) or (a).

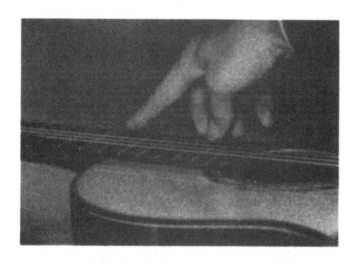

Figure 3

Figure 4

60

Study the following example, first using (p), then (a) to sound the harmonics: Right hand harmonics sound one octave higher than usual guitar notation.

a.

A harmonic and a bass note are sometimes played together.

(a) is used to sound the harmonic and (p) is used for the bass:

Right hand harmonics are generally not played below the 12th fret; they are often played above, at the 19th fret as in the following example:

Practice first with (p) then with (a).

d.

Artificial Harmonics

Artificial harmonics are those which are not found on an open string. Right hand harmonic technique is used to execute them and they are fingered in the conventional manner with the left hand.

Artificial harmonics are formed by touching the string one octave higher than the note formed with the left hand. Since the 12th fret is one octave above the open string, all octaves are produced the same number of frets above the 12th fret as the left hand note is above the nut, for example:

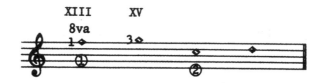

F is one fret above the nut so the string is touched at the first fret above the 12th fret. G is found at the third fret above the nut so the string is touched at the third fret above the 12th.

Practice the following scale exercises employing both artificial and natural harmonics. Right hand harmonic technique is used throughout; first with (p), then with (a):

a.

b.

Arpeggios in harmonics:

c.

Accompanied melody in harmonics:

d.

62

Carillon

The first four and last three measures of harmonics should be sounded with (p); all other harmonics must be sounded with (a).

The bass notes and inner voices are played with (p), very softly in order not to obscure the delicate melody in harmonics.

G. Yeatman

Andantino M.M. ♩ = 92

A Harmonic as the Highest Note of a Triad

The same right hand technique is used as above except that (m) sounds the inner voice:

Pastorale, by Carcassi, contains one note which may be unfamiliar: B, as occurs on the 2nd and 3rd beats of the fourth measure is found on the 1st string at the 7th fret.

Notice the harmonics in measures 8 and 24.

THE KEY OF D MAJOR

The key signature of D Major consists of two sharps, F♯ and C♯.

The following D Major scalewise progression of notes is played entirely in the *second position*. This is made possible by the fact that no 1st fret notes appear in the key of D Major; although playing in the second position, *open strings* must still be used.

Waltz Etude

All scale passages rest-stroke; arpeggio passages, as at measures 1, 3, 5, etc., free-stroke. Measure 17 (marked *) is the only exception; although the melody line is an arpeggio, it is played rest-stroke.

The Primary Chords—Key of D Major

As was the case in G Major, only the dominant group of chord formations in each new major key are unfamiliar.

The I or Tonic D Major chord below was V in the key of G.

The IV or Subdominant G in this key was I in G.

The new V or Dominant chords are A and A7.

Triads:

Basic Chord Formations

Ex. 32

Ex. 33

Root Position and Inversions of the Three Principal Chords

Triads:

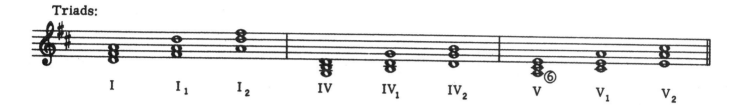

Four-voiced Chord Formations:

Although the inversions of I and IV have been studied in another key, they are presented here for the purpose of review and to acquaint the student, both by sound and by formation, with their new positions in this key.

The V7 (first inversion A7) is usually very difficult for students of this level and will not be included in the initial exercises.

It is recommended that the V chords be learned first; the V7 chords will then be easy to study through association.

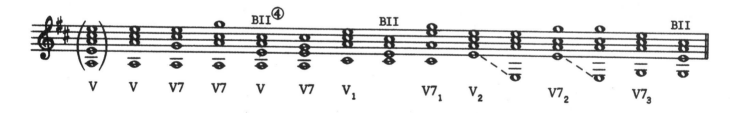

Ex. 34

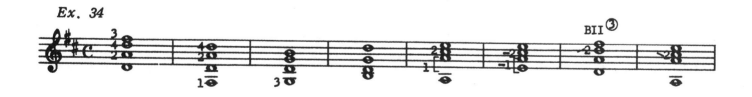

Ex. 35

Rhythm patterns for studying the above:

The following exercises employing inversions generally require considerable study for students at this level. If they are found to be too difficult, the student may defer their study until a later stage of development.

Ex. 36

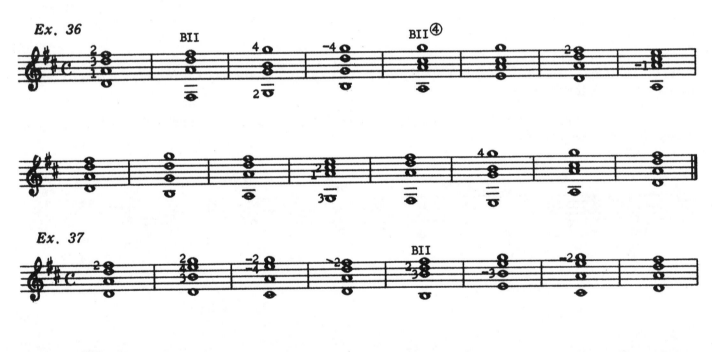

Ex. 37

Rhythm forms for studying the above:

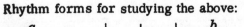

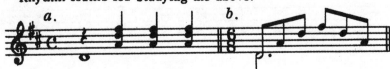

This *Waltz*, by Carulli, employs a fingering which may be unfamiliar but is often used for larger pieces: (i) and (a) are used to sound two notes together on adjacent strings. The notes between measures will then flow smoothly; (m) sounds the last 16th note in the measure, leaving (i) and (a) prepared to sound the chord. Since there are no quick notes in the last two sections of the piece, the conventional (i—m) combination is used.

Waltz

Andantino

F. Carulli

Prelude in D Major

G. Yeatman

Moderato

72

Allegretto

Rest-stroke is used for the melody whenever practical. Notice that short passages requiring repeated free-stroke are played entirely free-stroke.

M.M. ♩.= 63

F. Sor

THE LOW "D" TUNING

Many compositions are written or arranged for the guitar which require
the note D, one whole-step lower than the conventional 6th string tuned to E:

The notes on the low D-6 string are easily learned by observing two particulars:

1. The notes have the same names but are one octave lower than those on the D-4th string.

    Notes on the D-6th string (Key of D):

2. Since the string is tuned one whole-step lower, each note is found one whole-step (two
    frets) higher than when the string is tuned to E.

In order, therefore, to tune the 6th string to D, depress the string at the 7th fret instead
of the usual 5th fret; when played with the 5th string this will produce a unison A if tuned
accurately.

Chords with the 6th String Tuned to D

Root Position and Inversions:

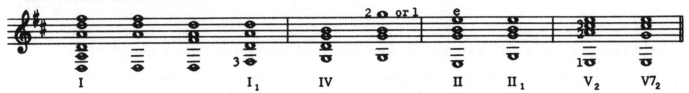

I   I₁   IV   II   II₁   V₂   V7₂

Ex. 41

Ex. 42

Ex. 43

Arietta

Moderato M.M. ♩. = 50 or ♪ = 152
(All melody, including harmonics in last 8 measures, REST-STROKE; basses, FREE-STROKE)

A.S.

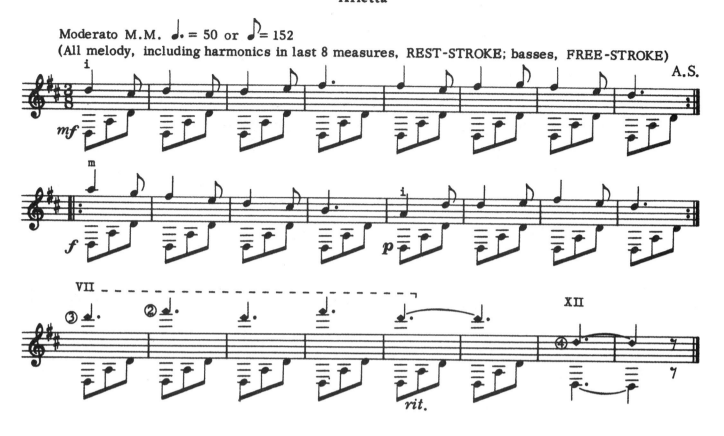

Andante

M.M. ♩ = 76

A. Diabelli

Danza

Allegretto M.M. ♩. = 50
(All melody REST-STROKE, bass FREE-STROKE)

A.S.

Harm. XII

THE KEY OF A MAJOR

The following two-octave A Major scale requires a shift to the second position on the 1st string. Observe left fingering very carefully:

The key signature consists of the THREE SHARPS, F#, C#, and G#:

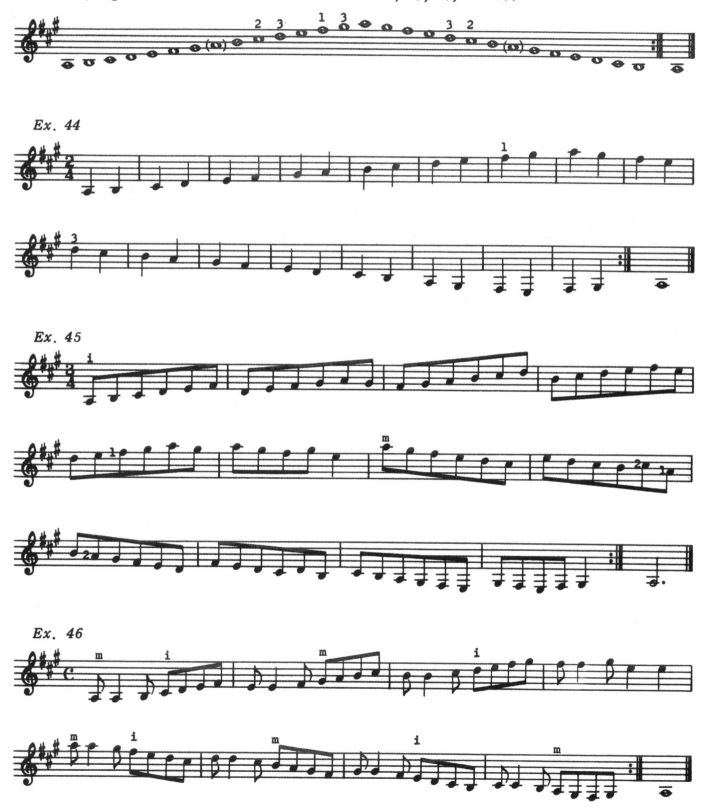

Ex. 44

Ex. 45

Ex. 46

78

Etude

Andante M.M. ♩ = 72

D. Aguado

The Primary Chords—Key of A Major

The primary chords in the key of A Major have previously been presented in other keys.

The I or tonic, A Major Chord was V in the key of D.

The IV or subdominant, D Major was V in G and I in D.

The V or dominant chords, E and E7, are also dominant in the key of A Minor.

Although the chords are familiar in other keys the student should firmly establish, by sound and feel, their new relationship in the key of A Major.

Basic Chord Formations

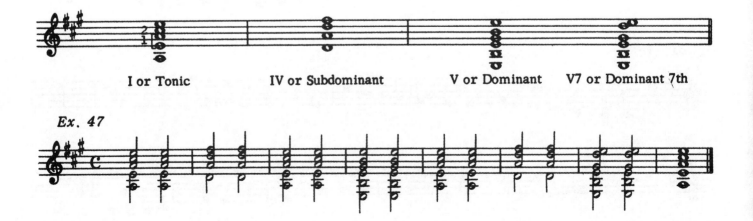

I or Tonic   IV or Subdominant   V or Dominant   V7 or Dominant 7th

Ex. 47

Root Position and Inversions of the Three Principal Chords

Four-voiced Chord Formations: CAREFULLY REVIEW ALL CHORDS!
Observe new fingering for first inversion D Major and first inversion E7.

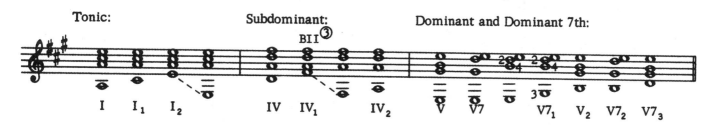

Highest note on the 2nd string:

Ex. 48

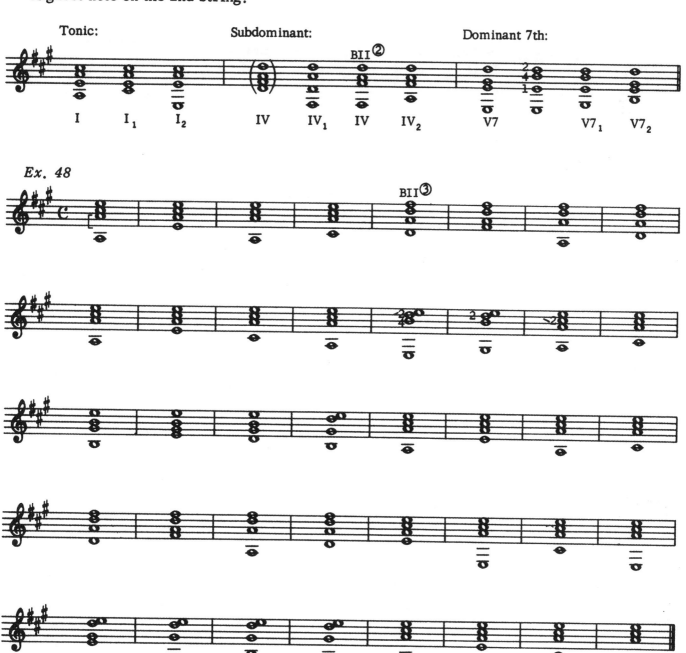

Ex. 49

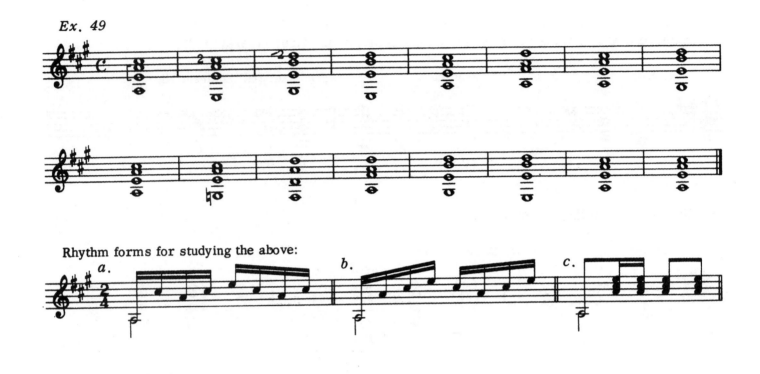

Rhythm forms for studying the above:

Two Short Pieces by A. Cano

Adagio

M.M. ♩ = 63 (All FREE-STROKE)

Andante

Since the basic primary chord formations in the key of A have already been learned, the student will find it interesting to proceed with new chord formations.

It is a commonly accepted fact that we learn best by associating that which is unfamiliar with that which is already known. The two chord formations which follow may be associated with two chords previously learned:

The new A Major formation is the same as G Major moved up the fingerboard one whole-step; this necessitates a change in fingering but the relative position of notes within the chord are the same. The BII③ now replaces the nut and the bass (root) of the chord is found on an open string.

The new E7 formation is the same as D7 moved up the fingerboard one whole-step. Again the fingering is changed so that the 1st finger replaces the nut.

Movable Chord Formations

This method of associating "open-string" chords with those where the 1st finger replaces the nut is a very practical procedure for finding chord formations in higher positions. Most 1st position chords employing open strings which can be fingered without the use of the 1st finger can be moved upwards on the fingerboard to produce chords in different keys; the 1st finger, of course, replaces the nut. The student may have observed how E Major is moved up in this manner to produce F Major, and that D Major is the 2nd inversion C Major triad moved up one whole-step, with an open string root in the bass.

Any chord which has no open string is known as a "movable chord formation", i.e., it may be moved up or down the fingerboard as required for different keys and chord progressions. The student should experiment with "open string" formations already learned and find new movable chord formations in higher positions. This procedure is an excellent left hand development study and will increase considerably one's general knowledge of the fingerboard.

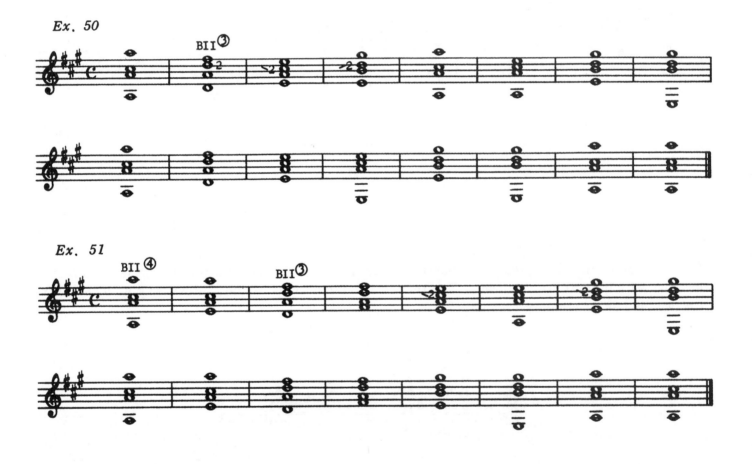

Ex. 50

Ex. 51

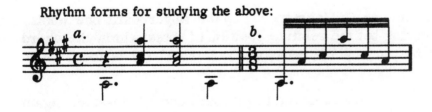

Rhythm forms for studying the above:

Waltz Allegro

M.M. ♩.=54 or ♪=162

M. Carcassi

The first two sections involving arpeggios, all FREE-STROKE. The last section consisting of scale passages, all REST-STROKE.

Fine

D.C. al Fine

The following *Beguine* by Yeatman, begins with two notes marked with fermatas (see page 42). Note the accent marks (>) throughout the piece. Remember: A wavy line placed at the left of a chord, as in the last two measures, means that it should be played broken or arpeggiated. Observe the key change at the end of the second ending and again just before the D.S. (D.S. ℅ al ⊕ e poi la Coda, means to repeat from the sign ℅ to the sign ⊕ and then play the Coda.)

Beguine

G. Yeatman

THE KEY OF E MAJOR

The key signature of E Major consists of four sharps, F♯, C♯, G♯, and D♯. Two full octaves of the E Major Scale are available in the 1st position:

Ex. 54

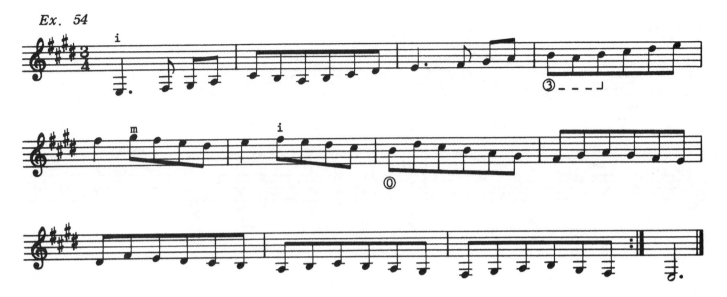

Moderato

Observe the F double sharp (✕) on the 3rd beat of the 11th measure. This raises the note a half step above the sharped tone.

M.M. ♪ = 112

M. Carcassi

The Primary Chords—Key of E Major

As was the case in the key of A Major, the primary chords in the key of E Major also have previously been presented in other keys.

The I or tonic, E Major Chord was V in the key of A Minor and A Major.

The IV or subdominant, A Major Chord was V in D and I in A.

The V or dominant chords, B and B7, are also Dominant in the key of E Minor.

Spare no effort to become thoroughly acquainted with the new relationship of these chords in the key of E Major:

Basic Chord Formations

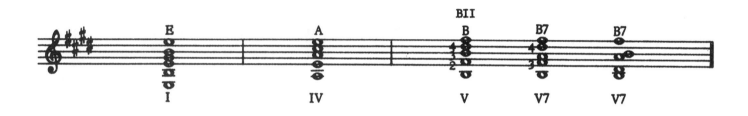

Since the E and A Major root position and inversions have been studied in two previous keys, only the B and B7 formations will be presented here: (The 1st inversion B Major, played in the 4th position is shown for the sake of completeness and will not be included in the exercises which follow.)

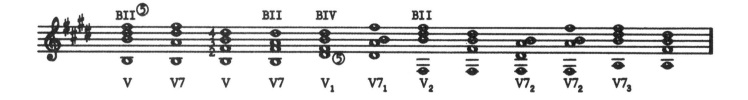

88

Ex. 56

Ex. 57

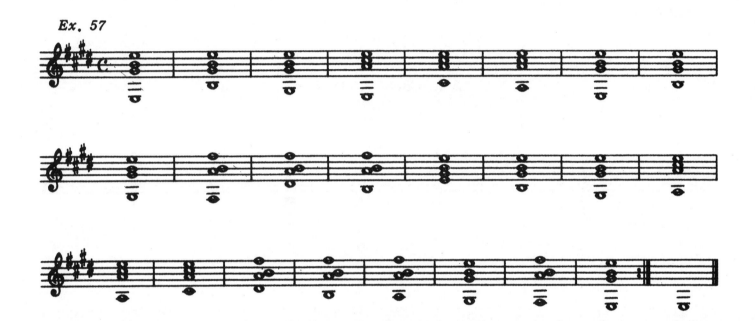

Rhythm forms:

Andante

M.M. ♩ = 76
(All FREE-STROKE)

F. Carulli

Waltz

Allegro M.M. ♩ = 132

M. Carcassi

Fine

D.C. al Fine

Rio De Noche

THE KEY OF F MAJOR

The key of F Major is not one of the most congenial keys to the guitar and is used much less frequently than the keys previously presented. However, its relative minor, D Minor, is a very practical key for the guitar and is commonly found in the repertory of the instrument. Before studying the key of D minor it is necessary of course, for the student to become acquainted with the key of F Major.

The key signature of F Major consists of one flat: B♭.

The Primary Chords—Key of F Major

The I or tonic F Major chord was IV in the key of C Major.

The IV or subdominant chord is Bb Major.

The V or dominant C Major chord was I in C Major; the V7 is a new formation.

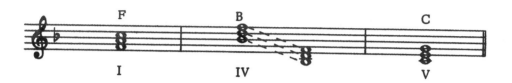

Basic Chord Formations

The IV or subdominant Bb Major chord formation is the same as B Major (V in E) moved downward one half-step, from the 2nd fret to the 1st.

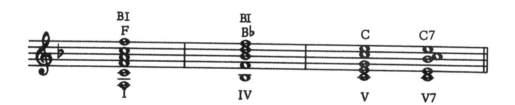

Ex. 60

Root Position and Inversions of the Three Principal Chords

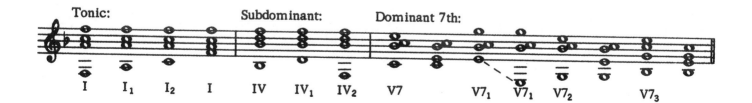

94

Ex. 61

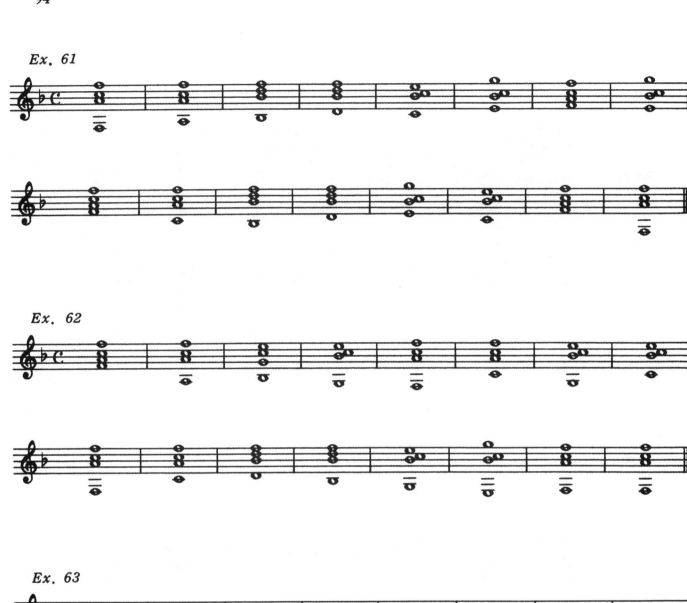

Ex. 62

Ex. 63

Rhythm forms:

Danza

A. Diabelli

March

96

Moderato

F. Sor

M.M. ♩. = 50

Etude in F Major

Allegro M.M. ♩ = 88

M. Giuliani

THE KEY OF D MINOR
(Relative to F Major)

D Melodic Minor Scale:

Ex. 64

Ex. 65

D Harmonic Minor Scale:

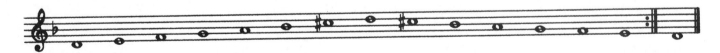

Ex. 66

Miniature Tarantella

M.M. ♩. = 72 to 84

A.S.

The Primary Chords—Key of D Minor

The I or tonic D Minor chord was IV in the key of A Minor

The IV or subdominant chord is G Minor.

The V and V7 dominant chords, A and A7, are also dominant in the key of D Major.

Triads:

Basic Chords Formations

Root Position and Inversions of the Three Primary Chords

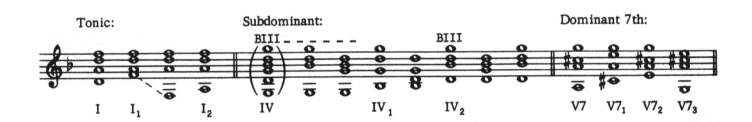

Caprice

M. Carcassi

Allegretto M.M. ♩ = 72 to 84

Considerable study is usually required to perform the following *Allegretto* at a lively, effective tempo. Carefully observe fingering for both hands.

Allegretto

NOTES IN THE HIGHER POSITIONS

This section deals with notes at the fifth fret and above—the student will have learned the first four frets from previous study. The higher notes must be learned both in notation and on the fingerboard; the technique of *shifting* is indispensable for their performance, and must be thoroughly developed.

1st String Notes in the Higher Positions

Although the student may have learned the higher notes on the 1st string in beginning slur studies, they are presented here both for review and as a contribution toward greater fluency in reading notes above the staff.

In the beginning give special attention to the half-step and whole-step arrangement of natural notes on the string. The half-steps, B-C and E-F can be considered guide-posts from which to gauge distance upward and downward.

Practice the following exercises, *naming each note* until all are thoroughly learned. HOLD 1st FINGER DOWN THROUGHOUT EACH EXERCISE.

Ex. 68

Ex. 69

The Guide-Finger Principle in Shifting

In studying scale passages requiring long shifts by the left hand it is most important to accustom oneself to using a *guide-finger*. This technique should be so thoroughly developed that its use becomes second nature. When practiced correctly, this manner of shifting gives the performer a feeling of assurance and is helpful in developing accuracy.

Observe the following points in shifting either upward or downward:

1. Permit the 1st L.H. finger to glide lightly along the string precisely to the fret establishing the position for playing the notes involved.

2. The 1st finger glides directly to the fret establishing the position even though the note at that fret is not immediately played. This often occurs in downward shifts when the 4th, 3rd, or 2nd finger plays the first note in the new position. (See Examples 1, 3, and 4 below.) It may also occur in shifting upward, in which case the note held by the 1st finger may not be played at all. (See Examples 2 and 3 below.)

3. Release pressure upon the string just enough so that it does not contact frets producing a *glissando*, "sliding", effect during the shift.

4. The left thumb *must not drag behind the hand* during either the upward or downward shift. Release pressure for an instant so that the thumb will slide along the neck to maintain the same position relative to the fingers at all times.

5. Observe *glide marks*, ╱ or ╲ (either upward or downward), indicating *guide fingers*.

Example 1. From position V to X to V

Example 2. V to IX to V

1st fin-
ger to V

1st finger must glide up to IX, although
it is not used in playing a note there.

Example 3. V to VII to V

Example 4. VII to X to VII

1st fin-
ger to VII

1st fin-
ger to V

1st fin-
ger to VII

Ex. 70

The following exercise necessitates an extension of the 4th finger one half-step upward out of the normal eighth position; DO NOT SHIFT TO NINTH POSITION. The reach of one whole-step between the 3rd and the 4th fingers is quite common especially in higher positions where the frets are closer together; practice until performance is easy and fluent.

Ex. 71

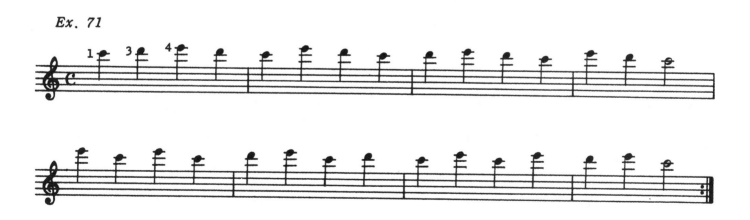

The Accidental:

Ex. 72

Through a thorough study of the guide-finger principle the performer will eventually develop the ability to sense automatically the distance of the shift required. This development is obviously an absolute necessity in learning to read fluently. Either one or any combination of the four fingers may be used as guide-fingers up or down the fingerboard. The 1st finger glide, however, is of particular importance in performing scalewise passages on one string; proceed as follows:

1. Think in terms of half and whole-steps (distance of one or two frets).
2. Listen intently and concentrate upon the sound and feel of the interval.
3. Release pressure between thumb and finger just enough so that both members may shift in unison as previously explained under "The Guide-Finger Principle In Shifting".
4. Once the exercise is begun, *keep eyes on music*. Train the fingers to find their way through practicing as instructed in item number 2.
5. Practice slowly at first to develop accuracy. Gradually increase tempo and play all exercises in eighth notes.

The Half-Step Shift

Ex. 73

Ex. 74

1st and 2nd fingers glide downward simultaneously during shift.

Alternating 1st and 4th finger glide: The complete shift must be executed during 4th finger glide. Guard against tendency of the 4th finger to extend upward before the actual shift is made.

Ex. 75

The Whole-Step Shift

Ex. 76

1st finger glides upward.   1st and 2nd fingers glide downward simultaneously.

Ex. 77

Ex. 78

One and One-Half Step Shift

(Three Frets)

Ex. 79

Ex. 80

The Shift of Two Whole Steps

(Four Frets)

Ex. 81

Ex. 82

The Shift of Two and One-Half Steps
(Five Frets)

This is the longest shift encountered in diatonic scale passages. Since the two and one-half step shift occurs frequently in music containing extended scale passages, fluent accuracy and speed in its execution are of utmost importance.

Train the ear to recognize the whole-step scalewise interval between the two tones occurring immediately before and after the shift.

Ex. 83

The following exercise is excellent for developing the technique of shifting. Memorize the pattern and practice with these points in mind:

1. Check left arm and hand form; arm relaxed downward, wrist relatively straight, fingers curved.

2. Aim for a sensation of relaxation throughout hand and arm even during the most rapid shift. This, of course, requires a high degree of coordination which can be developed only through much thorough repetition.

3. Check the tempo with a metronome to be sure that no hesitation occurs during the shift. Finally play in slow triplets.

110

Ex. 84

Shifting in Major Scales

The following major scales should be practiced slowly at an even tempo. Increase tempo and play in eighth notes, and finally in triplets—but only when accuracy is assured.

Play and name and even better, *sing* each note until the scales are memorized. In this manner, both key feeling and shifting sense are established in mind and hands.

In order to form one full octave of the G Major scale on the 1st string, two new notes, high F♯ and G, are introduced.

111

Scale No. 4   G Major

Frets: XIV XV

F♯   G

Scale No. 5   D Major

Scale No. 6   A Major, with two new notes, high G♯ and A (see Fig. 6)
Frets: XIV XVI XVII

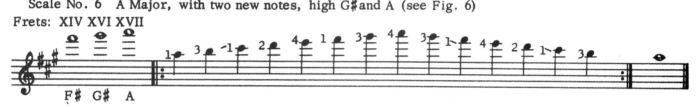

F♯   G♯   A

Scale No. 7   E Major

Fig. 5. Lean slightly to the left and drop left shoulder to facilitate fingering in high positions.

112

Adagio Waltz

Melody entirely on the 1st string.

M.M. ♩ = 63

A.S.

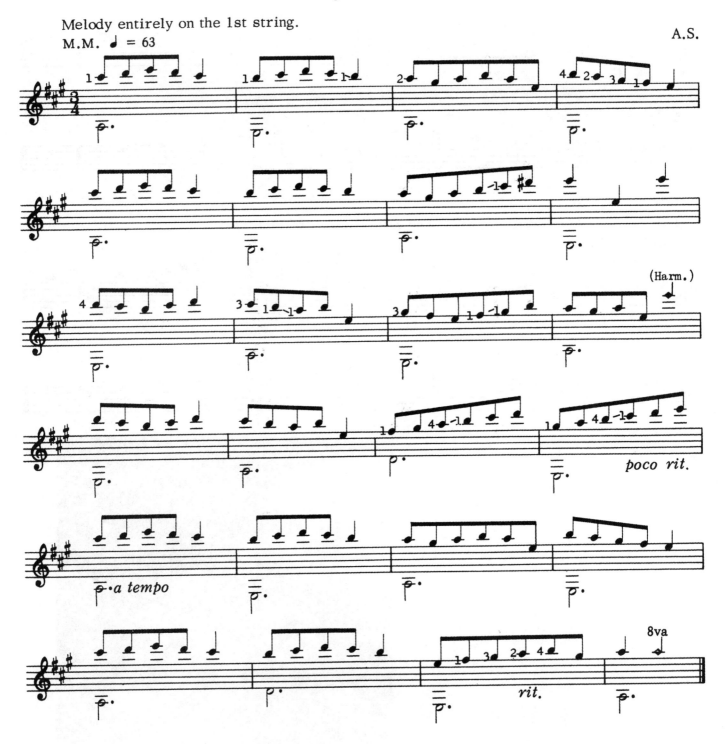

Two Lessons from the Guitar Method by F. Sor (1778—1839)
Lesson No. 6 in C Major

Scale Exercise:

Begin very slowly, practice shifts separately until accurate; all free-stroke.

Moderato M.M. ♩ = 108

poco rit.

114

While studying the Sor Lessons, the student should proceed to the following exercises for learning notes on the 2nd string. This procedure provides a balanced study of pieces and exercises for learning the fingerboard; a similar approach should be used for studying the remaining strings.

Lesson No. 12 in A Minor

2nd String Notes in the Higher Positions

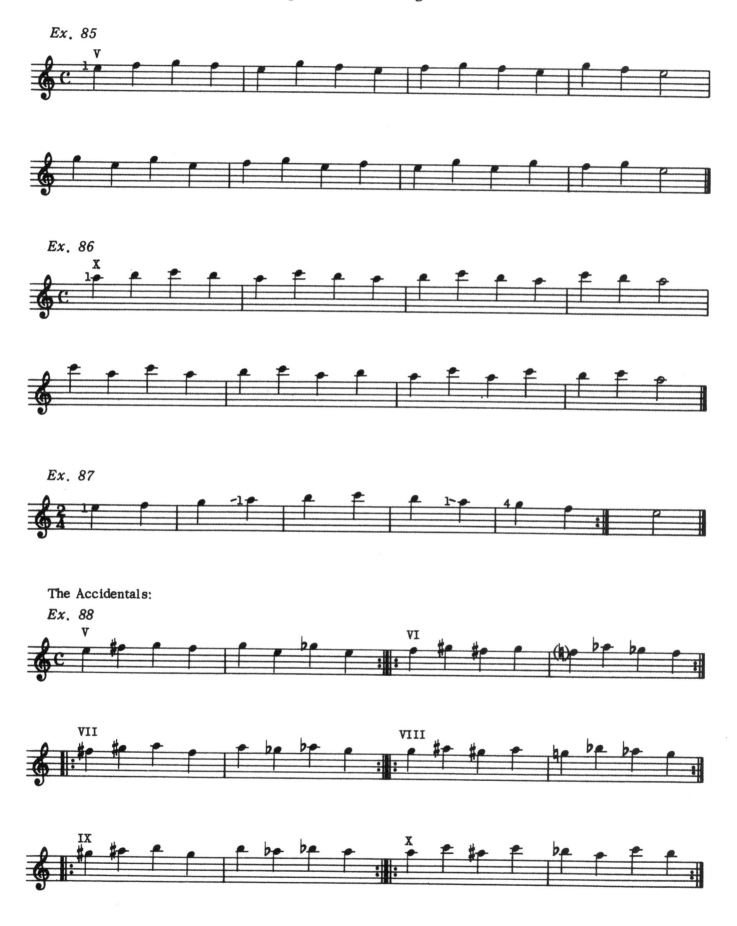

Major Scales

(Covering Higher Positions on the Second String)

No. 1   C Major

No. 2   G Major

No. 3   G Major Extended

No. 4   D Major (Incomplete)

No. 5   A Major

No. 6   E Major (Incomplete)

No. 7   B Major

No. 8   B♭ Major

No. 9   E♭ Major (Incomplete)

No. 10   A♭ Major

Position Exercises—1st and 2nd Strings

The next step in learning the fingerboard in the higher positions is to consider the scale relationship of notes on the first two strings in each position.

The following twelve exercises cover six positions (IV through IX) on the 1st and 2nd strings. The two most suitable major keys are presented in each position. The keys having less complicated key signatures are presented first in their proper positions, followed by the more difficult keys. Since no shifts are necessary, left hand fingering is not included.

First name and play each note until fluent without strict regard to rhythm. Then count, using the metronome when necessary to maintain even tempo.

Fifth Position - C and F Major

Seventh Position - G and D Major

Ninth Position - A and E Major

118

Fourth Position - E and B Major

Ex. 95

Ex. 96

Sixth Position - D♭ and F♯ Major

Ex. 97

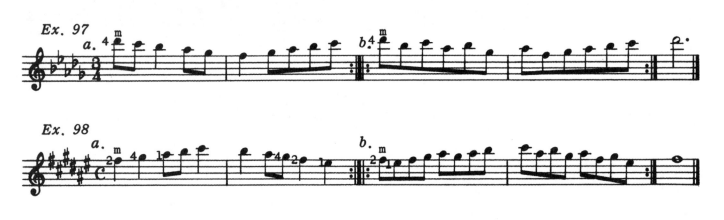

Ex. 98

Eighth Position - A♭ and E♭ Major

Ex. 99

Ex. 100

Scales in Thirds

(On the 1st and 2nd Strings)

Problems of fingering thirds:

The high degree of control required to execute several rapid shifts consecutively generates considerable tension throughout the left hand and arm, and makes it extremely difficult to play accurately and clearly. Extended consecutive shifts, therefore, should be eliminated or kept at a minimum especially in rapid passages. It is not generally recommended that more than two, or at most three, shifts be played consecutively.

The commonly used fingering of thirds shown below the staff in the following exercise, necessitates unbroken consecutive shifts upward and downward along the fingerboard. The recommended fingering is shown above the staff. The brief pause after each shift tends to eliminate tension and the undesirable glissando effect often heard in performances of consecutive thirds. There will be involved not only longer shifts but "across-fingerboard" fingering (i.e., lifting a finger and immediately placing it on an adjacent string), and the result will at first be a somewhat staccato effect. Concentrated practice will eliminate this. Shifts should be as rapid as possible, and the student should maintain a sense of relaxation at each stop along the fingerboard.

120

Andante

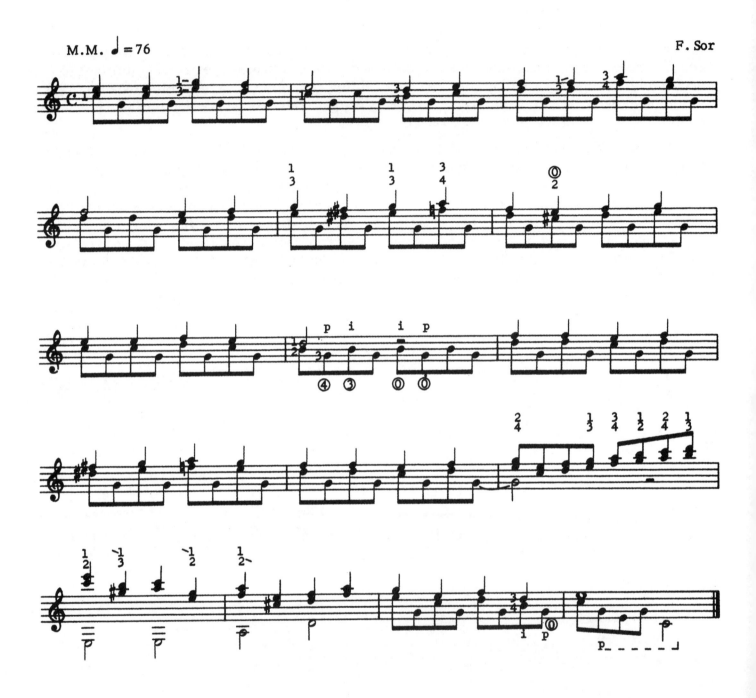

An Etude and Two Lessons from the Sor Method

Etude from Lesson No. 19

The 13th measure of the following piece contains the unfamiliar note, B, on the 6th string, seventh fret; carefully observe the fingering.

Lesson No. 13 in A Minor

122

Lesson No. 9 in A Major

Scale Exercise:

Allegretto M.M. ♩ = 108

3rd String Notes in the Higher Positions

Ex. 104

Ex. 105

Ex. 106

The Accidentals:

Ex. 107

Major Scales
(Covering Higher Positions on the Third String)

Scale No. 1   G Major

Scale No. 2   D Major

Scale No. 3   D Major Extended

Scale No. 4   E Major

Scale No. 5   F Major

Scale No. 6   E♭ Major

Scale No. 7   A♭ Major

Position Exercises—1st, 2nd and 3rd Strings

Each position of the fingerboard contains notes which form the basis for the major and relative minor scales of five keys (see the author's *Complete Scale Studies*). Inclusion of the 3rd string notes makes it practical to present the scalewise notes of the five *major* keys in the positions most suitable at this time. Because of the limited range of notes on three strings, only one formation contains a full octave of the major scale. Each exercise begins and ends on the tonic of the key, however, and along with other notes of the scale, establishes a definite "key feeling". Observe that the same relative formations of scalewise notes occur in each given position; only the keys change in progressing upward or downward along the fingerboard.

Fifth Position

Ex. 111 Bb Major

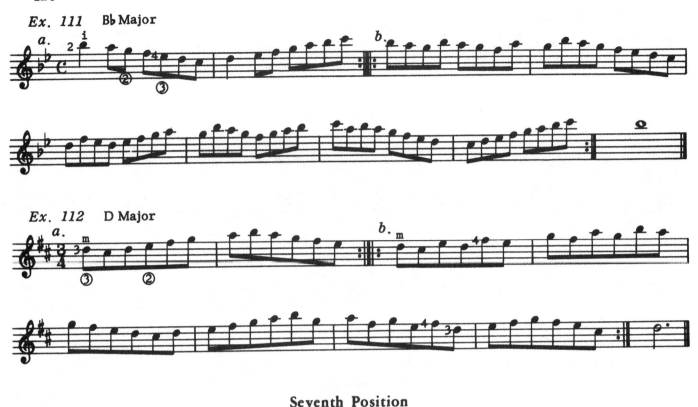

Ex. 112 D Major

Seventh Position

Ex. 113 C Major

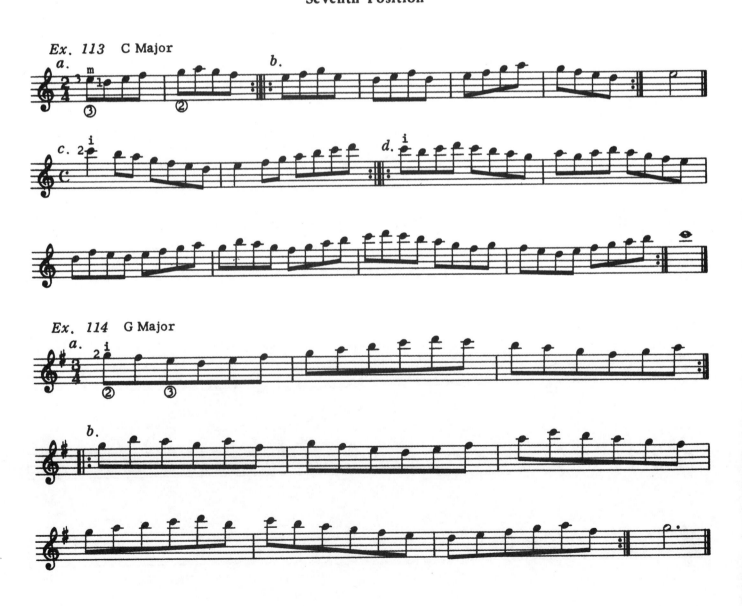

Ex. 114 G Major

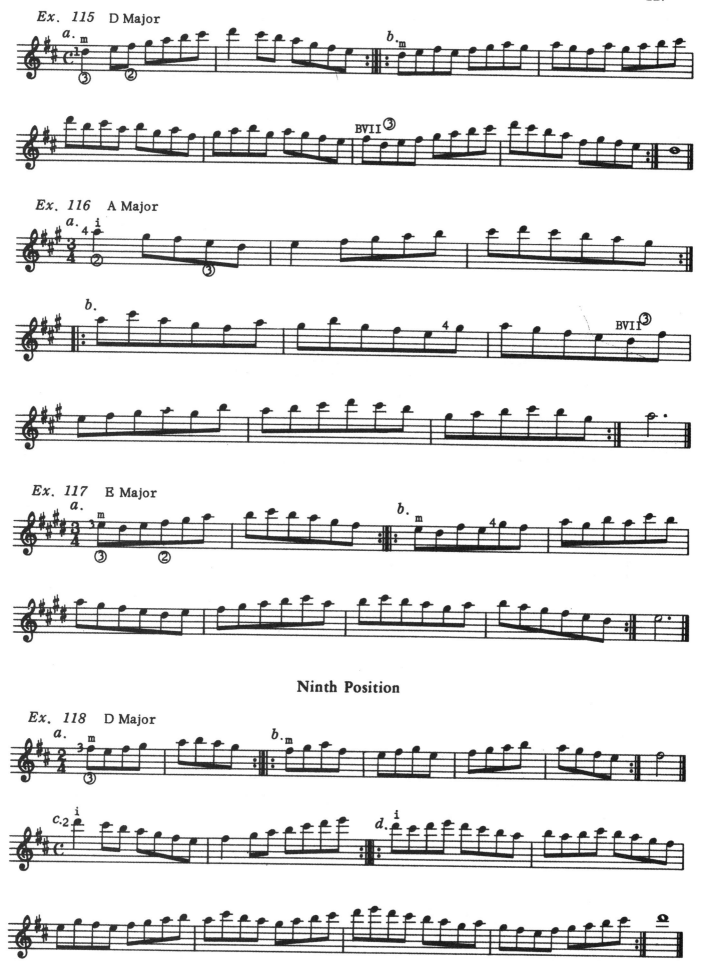

Ninth Position

Ex. 119   A Major

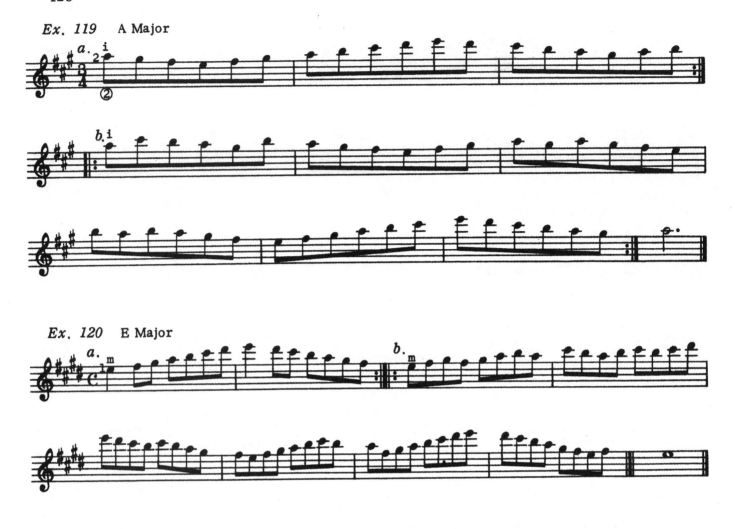

Ex. 120   E Major

Two Lessons from the Method by D. Aguado (1784-1849)

Both pieces have a wide range of effective performance tempos, as shown by the metronome marks.

Lesson No. 26

Lesson No. 40

M.M. ♩ = 66 to 88

4th String Notes in the Higher Positions

Major Scales
(Covering Higher Positions on the Fourth String)

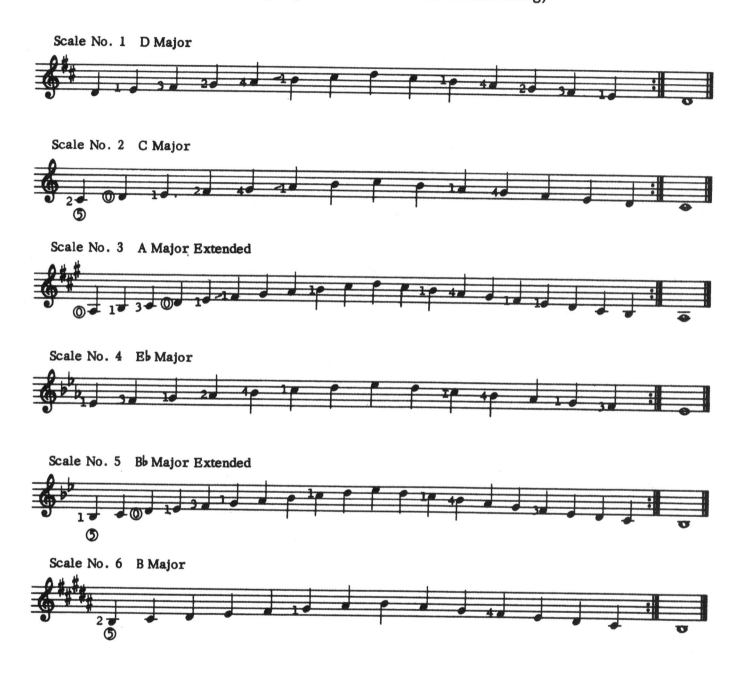

Position Exercises — First Four Strings

(The Squeeze Shift)

The next step in the study of major keys and scales across the fingerboard is the shift by contraction, commonly called the "squeeze shift". The squeeze shift involves the 1st and the 4th left hand fingers in a shift of one position either upward or downward. In the descending shift, the 4th finger contracts (or squeezes) downward one fret; in ascending, the 1st finger contracts upward one fret. In both instances, the finger *not* executing the squeeze holds as the other finger contracts toward it to be placed on the proper note. The left thumb may remain stationary in brief departures from the original position, as in the following examples:

Fluent execution of the squeeze shift is indispensable to the legato performance of rapid scales and scale patterns. Whenever it can be used, this shift is a very accurate and rapid means of performing the half step shift.

Fourth and Fifth Positions

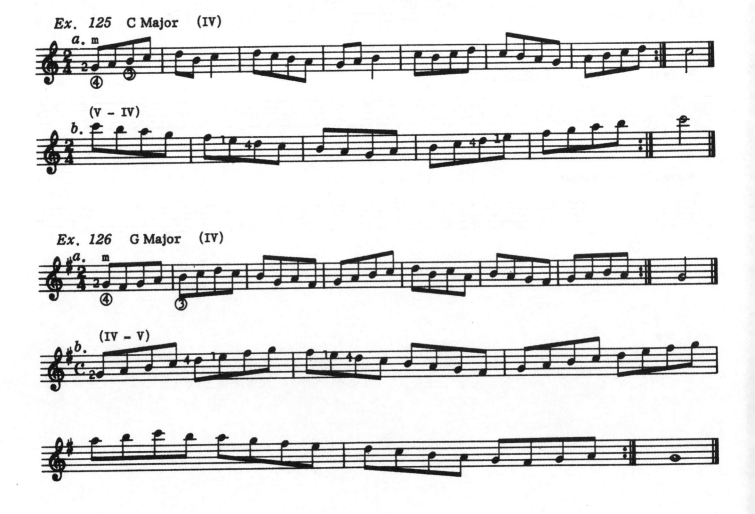

Ex. 127 Bb Major (V)

a.

b. (V)

Sixth and Seventh Positions

Ex. 128 C Major (VII)

a.

b.

Ex. 129 D Major (VI)

a.

(VII – VI)

b.

Ex. 130 A Major (VI)

a.

(VI – VII)

b.

134

Ninth and Tenth Positions

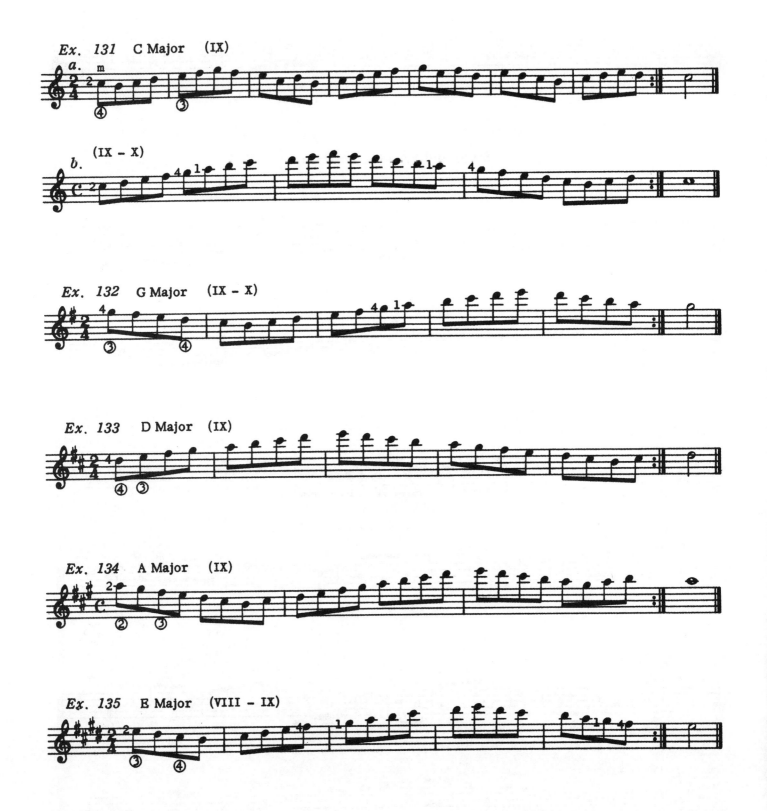

Ex. 131   C Major   (IX)

a.

b.   (IX – X)

Ex. 132   G Major   (IX – X)

Ex. 133   D Major   (IX)

Ex. 134   A Major   (IX)

Ex. 135   E Major   (VIII – IX)

Two Lessons from the Aguado Method

Lesson No. 17— Aguado

Lesson No. 38

5th String Notes in the Higher Positions

Ex. 136

Ex. 137

Ex. 138

All the Accidentals:
Ex. 139

Major Scales
(Covering Higher Positions on the Fifth String)

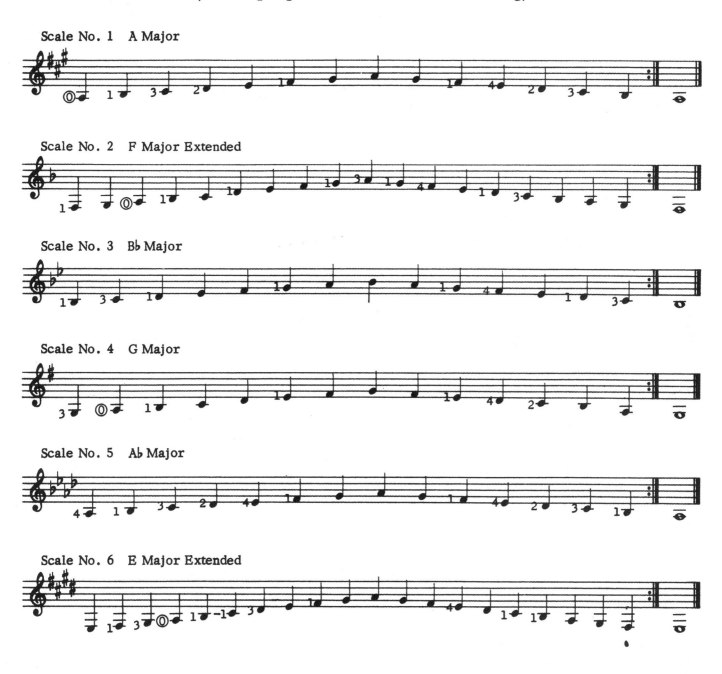

Scale No. 1   A Major

Scale No. 2   F Major Extended

Scale No. 3   Bb Major

Scale No. 4   G Major

Scale No. 5   Ab Major

Scale No. 6   E Major Extended

Position Exercises — 1st through 5th Strings

Ex. 140   D Major   (IV)

(IV – V)

138

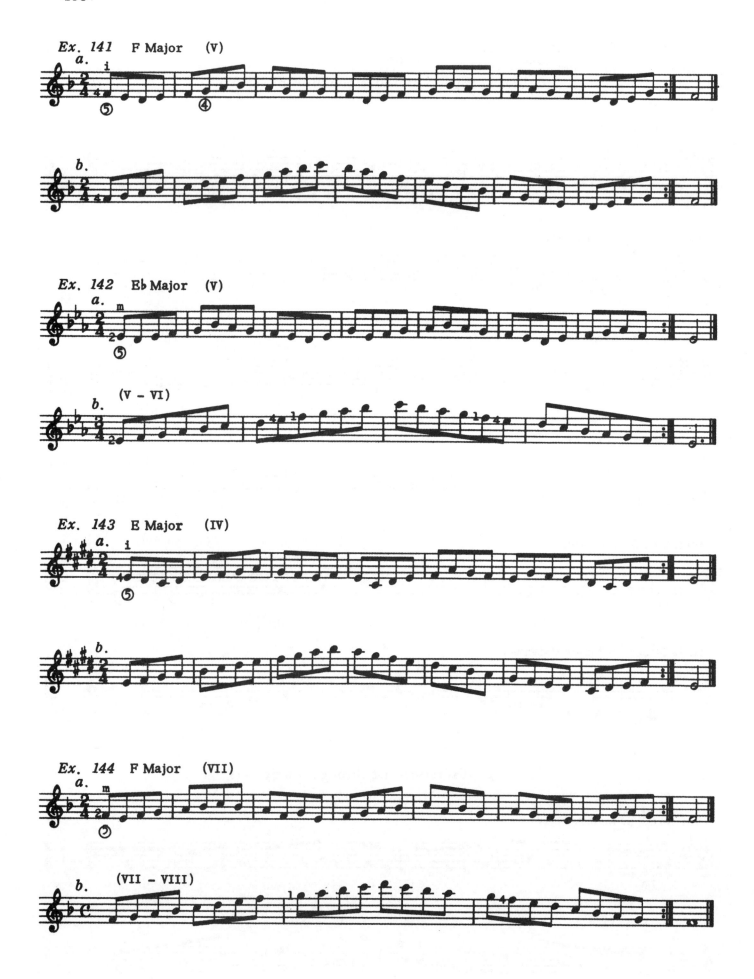

139

Two Lessons from the Aguado Method

Lesson No. 24

Lesson No. 28

6th String Notes in the Higher Positions

142

Major Scales

(Covering Higher Positions on the Sixth String)

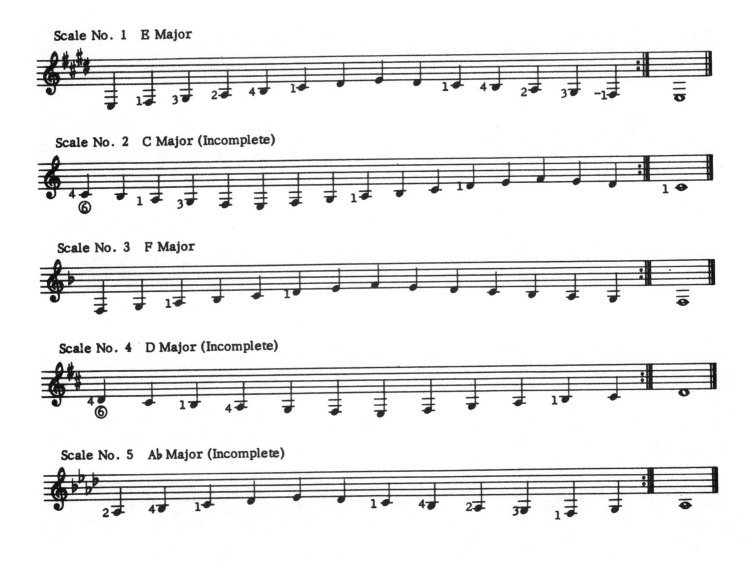

Position Exercises—6th and 5th Strings

Ex. 155   Bb Major   (V)

Ex. 156   C Major   (VII)

Ex. 157   D Major   (IX)

Ex. 158   E Major   (IX)

Ex. 159   B Major   (VI)

Ex. 160   Eb Major   (VIII)

Ex. 161   Db Major   (VIII)

Position Scale Formations—Major

The following five basic scale formations on the fingerboard are presented in the keys which for the most part occur in the seventh position. Three of the scale formations necessitate brief excursions into adjacent positions using the "squeeze shift". All five, however, are referred to as seventh position scales, e.g., seventh position C Major scale, seventh position F Major scale, etc.

These scale forms may be moved to other positions on the fingerboard to play scales in all keys. No serious student of the guitar should neglect making a thorough study of the five major scale forms and their relative minors in all practical keys and positions. These scales form the basis for two and three octave scales covering the entire scope of the guitar fingerboard. (See the author's *Complete Scale Studies*.)

SUPPLEMENTARY PIECES

146

Andante

M.M. ♩ = 60

F. Sor

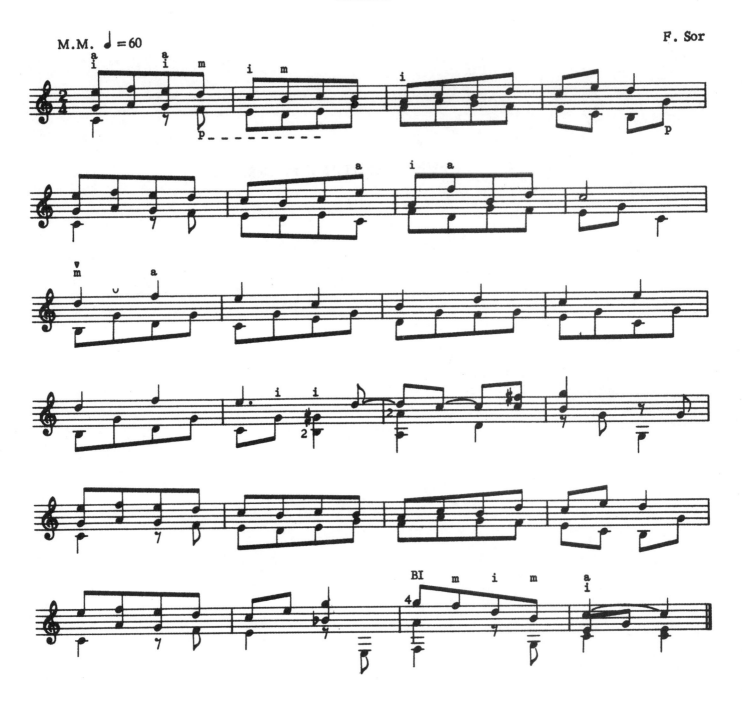

Lesson No. 13 — Aguado

Andante

M.M. ♩ = 88

M. Giuliani

Lesson No. 15—Aguado

Lesson No. 14— Aguado

M.M. ♪= 126

Vivace

M.M. ♩ = 76 to 100

M. Giuliani

Larghetto

M.M. ♩ = 56

F. Sor

poco rit.   *a tempo*

Minuetto

Andante M.M. ♩ = 76

F. Sor

Moderato

F. Sor

Lesson No. 10 — Sor

Lesson No. 29 — Aguado

Lesson No. 35 — Aguado

Allegro M.M. ♪ = 88 to 100

Two Preludes by F. Tarrega

Adagio

Andantino

Andantino M.M. ♩. = 52 (or ♪ = 156)